FLOWER WORLD VARIATIONS

A SEQUENCE OF SONGS FROM THE YAQUI DEER DANCE

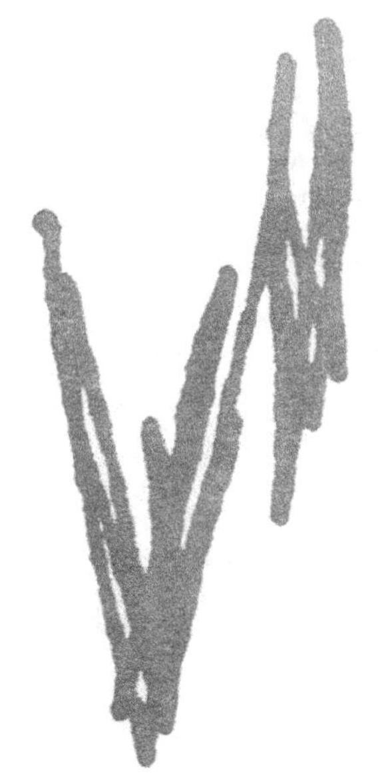

EXPANDED EDITION

POEMS BY JEROME ROTHENBERG
DRAWINGS BY HAROLD COHEN

the operating system
brooklyn and worldwide
2017

the operating system print//document

FLOWER WORLD VARIATIONS

ISBN 978-1-946031-13-6
Library of Congress Control Number 2017951482

*This text was set in Minion, ARB-187 Moderne Caps, Science Fair, HeavyLOUDedgeline, Andale Mono,
and OCR-A Standard. Operating System books in limited edition and small run are printed and bound by
Spencer Printing, in Honesdale, PA, in the USA, with distribution to the trade and POD via Ingram.*

Original version: "15 Flower World Variations," ISBN # 0:87924-051-2, Membrane Press © 1984
Republished, redesigned and expanded upon with permission.

As of 2020 all of our titles are available for donation-only download via our Open Access Library:
http://www.theoperatingsystem.org/os-open-access-community-publications-library/

the operating system
141 Spencer Street #203
Brooklyn, NY 11205
www.theoperatingsystem.org
operator@theoperatingsystem.org

FLOWER WORLD VARIATIONS

15 flower world variations: a pre-face

The exciting thing about all this is that as it is new it is old & as it is old it is new, but now really we have come to be in our way which is an entirely different way.

(Gertrude Stein, from Narration)

The work as such goes back to the late 1970s, a time for me of exploration into the ethnopoetic sources of poetry & for Harold Cohen an investigation of the nature of artmaking/markmaking through a new computer technology & his pointed observations of marks left behind by the oldest "technicians of the sacred." In either case, to use Harold's words, what we were after, each in his own way, was "a sort of minimum configuration of deep-level behavioral mechanisms" as the basis for new work still to come – "from the Californian petroglyphs at one extreme to my own drawing at the other." It was that, with an abiding sense of friendship & kinship, that brought us together on a small book of poems with computer-generated drawings – not illustrations so much as testimony to a similarity of procedures & concerns. For this our vehicle was a book published by Karl Young's Membrane Press in the rough & tumble style of so much small press publication then – the images, all black & white, chosen from the drawings that Harold's program "Aaron" was already pouring out in great profusion. The combination of new & old was critical from both sides of our collaboration.

For this the starting point was a Yaqui Easter ceremony that I was privileged to witness in 1981 through the good offices of Anselmo Valencia, the leader of the New Pascua Pueblo in Tucson. Here the principal ceremonial presences – the sacred Deer Dancer & the Pascola Clowns – came from what the Yaquis called "flower world," "enchanted world" & "wilderness world," among the English terms used to describe the other-than-human domain surrounding the settled Yaqui villages: "a region of untamed things into which man's influence does not extend" (Edward Spicer). In mythic times that world (*huya aniya*) may have been *everything*, later reduced (so Spicer tells us) "to a specialized part of a larger whole, rather than the whole itself . . . . Not replaced, as the Jesuits would have wished ... it became the other world, the wild world surrounding the towns." Within the frame of a native & independent Catholicism, it persists in the present, into which it brings the mythic figures of Dancer & Clowns. The songs accompanying the very taut, very classical Deer Dance are, in their totality, an extraordinary example of traditional poesis: the cumulative construction by word & image of that Flower World from which the Dancer comes.

As a follow-up to that I turned to earlier ("literal") translations of some of those songs in Carleton S. Wilder's 1963 book *The Yaqui Deer Dance*, which presented me with the gist of what the songs were saying & some sense of how they were treated in actual performance. My intention, as with other "total translations" I was then attempting, was to compose poems in which all such features were immediately apparent, not only the meanings but the ways in which phrases repeated & reinforced each other between & within songs, so that the rhythms of the original Yaqui were present enough to create new forms & sounds in English. The proof of that of course was intended both for the written page & for subsequent performance – to lay bare in the process the fundamentals of poetry (*poesis*) wherever found.

It was a similar concern that Harold applied to his own work & to its relation to the petroglyphs we both observed on nearby cave & rock walls in southern California. And his own first move was to bring his new computer program to the same level of performance – labeled "primitive" but, as he noted, far from that – as a starter. "In other words," he wrote, "the choice of mechanisms [for programming the computer] was largely intuitive & arbitrary. I suspected that I would be on reasonably safe ground if I limited myself, at the outset at least, to what I assumed to be perceptual primitives, & I selected three: the ability to differentiate between figure & ground, to differen-

tiate between open forms & closed forms, & to dif-
ferentiate between insideness & outsideness." The
computer-generated drawings at that point were ab-
stract, though over time they would be programmed
to show "real-world"/ "flower world" images & often
dazzling colors, the cover image for the present
volume a wonderful example.

When Harold Cohen died a year ago the original
Flower World Variations had been out of print for
some time & the idea of bringing his new color
work into the mix had long been forgotten. It was
through the intervention of Lynne DeSilva-Johnson
& The Operating System that the idea of the pres-
ent volume emerged: an enhanced version of the
1984 edition, which it supplements with a color
cover & an essay/manifesto of Harold's that I pub-
lished at about the same time in *New Wilderness
Letter*, a magazine I had just started as the con-
tinuation of *Alcheringa Ethnopoetics*, an earlier
joint venture with the anthropologist & poet Den-
nis Tedlock. That it may also serve as a memorial
& tribute brings a certain sadness but a hope as
well of other things to come.

Jerome Rothenberg
Encinitas, California
May 2017

                The small nouns
Crying faith
In this in which the wild deer
Startle, and stare out.

                    —George Oppen

one

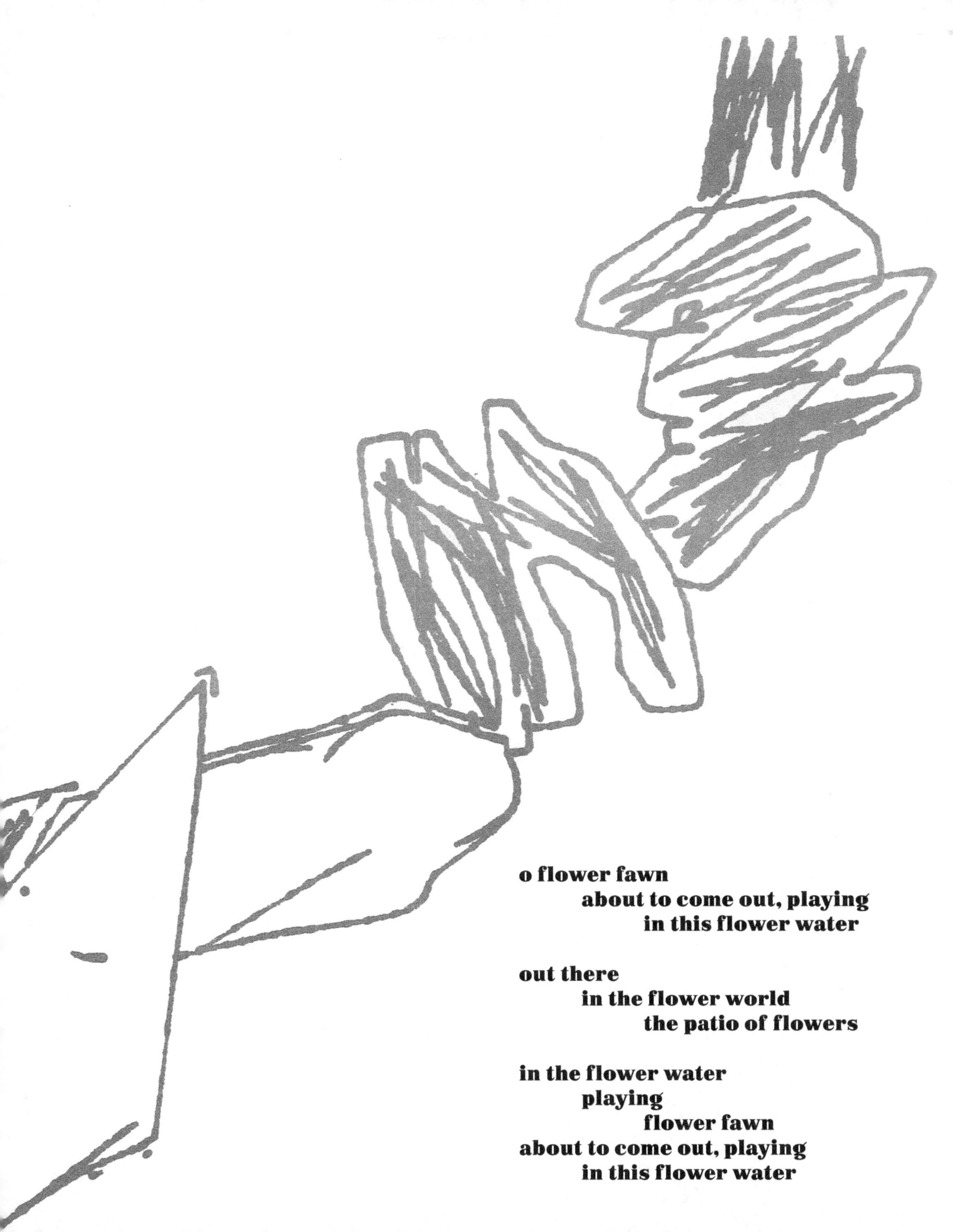

o flower fawn
        about to come out, playing
                in this flower water

out there
        in the flower world
                the patio of flowers

in the flower water
        playing
                flower fawn
about to come out, playing
        in this flower water

two

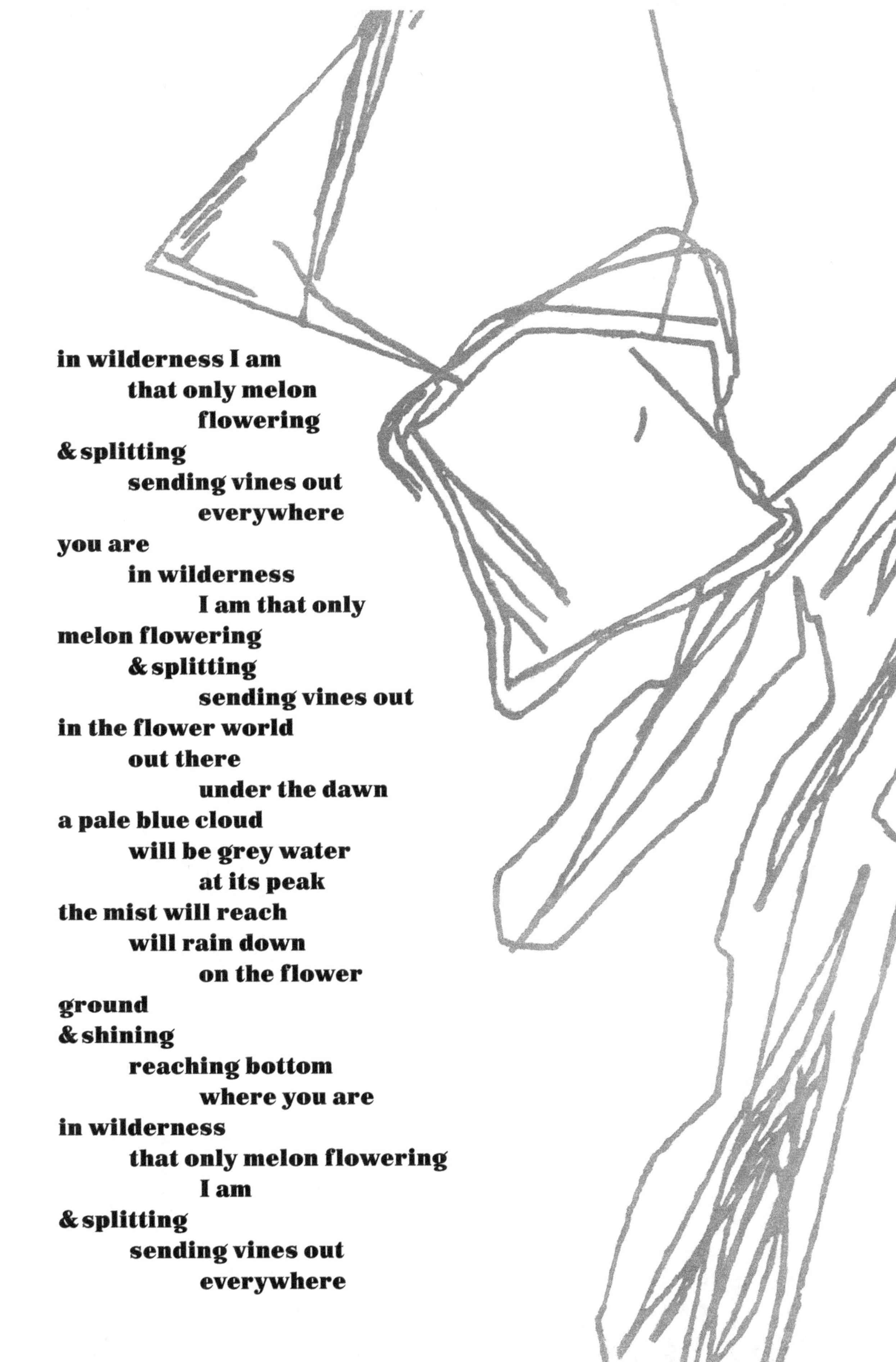

in wilderness I am
     that only melon
         flowering
& splitting
     sending vines out
         everywhere
you are
     in wilderness
         I am that only
melon flowering
     & splitting
         sending vines out
in the flower world
     out there
         under the dawn
a pale blue cloud
     will be grey water
         at its peak
the mist will reach
     will rain down
         on the flower
ground
& shining
     reaching bottom
         where you are
in wilderness
     that only melon flowering
         I am
& splitting
     sending vines out
         everywhere

three

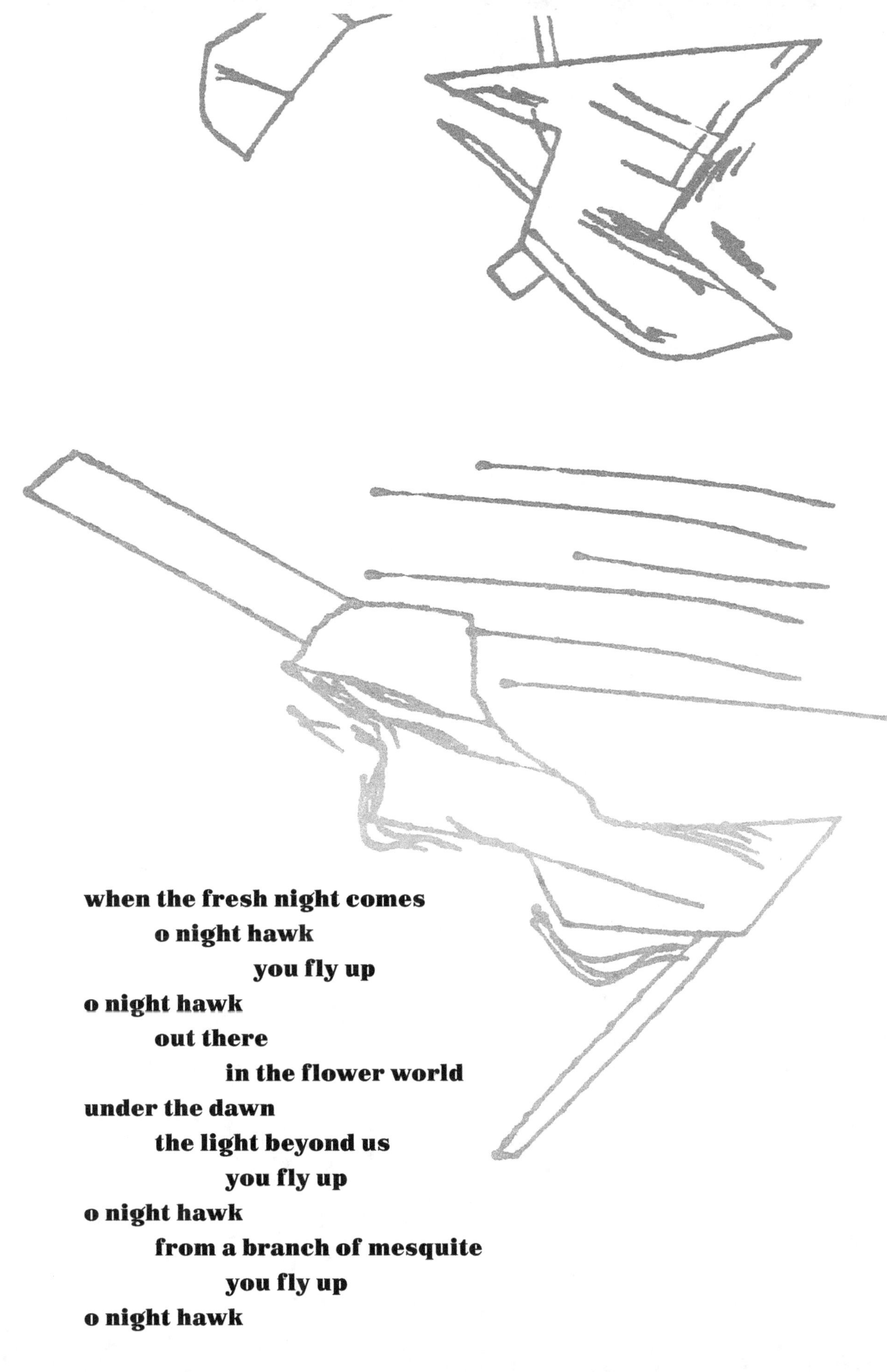

when the fresh night comes
    o night hawk
        you fly up
o night hawk
    out there
        in the flower world
under the dawn
    the light beyond us
        you fly up
o night hawk
    from a branch of mesquite
        you fly up
o night hawk

four

(where is the rotted stick that screeches lying?)
the screeching rotted stick is lying over there
(where is the rotted stick that screeches lying?)
the screeching rotted stick is lying over there
there in the flower world
                beyond us
                                in the tree world
the screeching rotted stick
                is lying
                                over there the screeching
rotted stick is lying
                over there

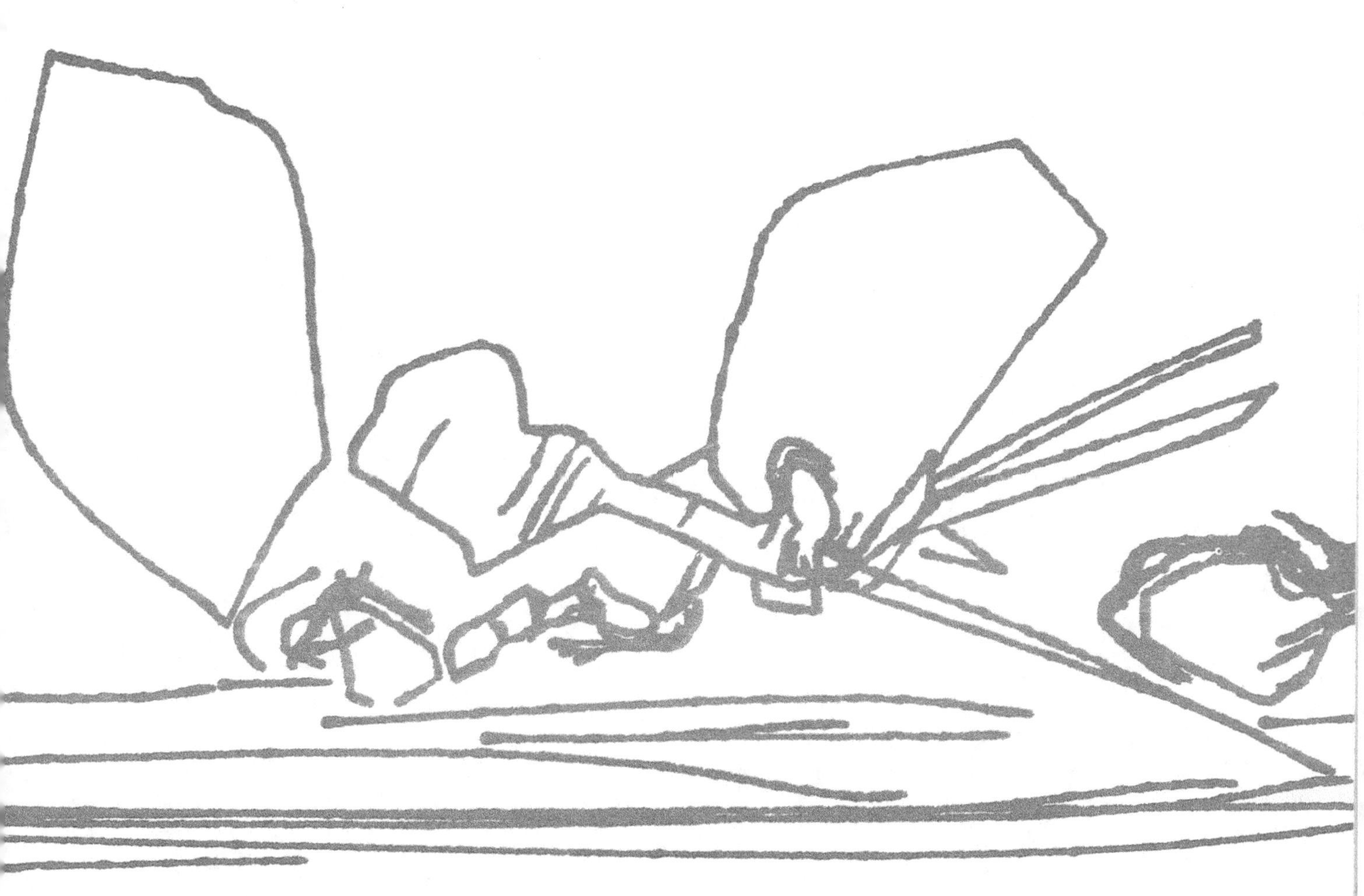

five

ah brother
        look at you
                a deer with flowers
brother
        shake your antlers
                little brother
shake your antlers
        deer with flowers
                why not let your belt
your deer hoofs
        shake? why not vibrate
                cocoons
strapped to your ankles
        brother
                shake them
little brother
        shake & roll

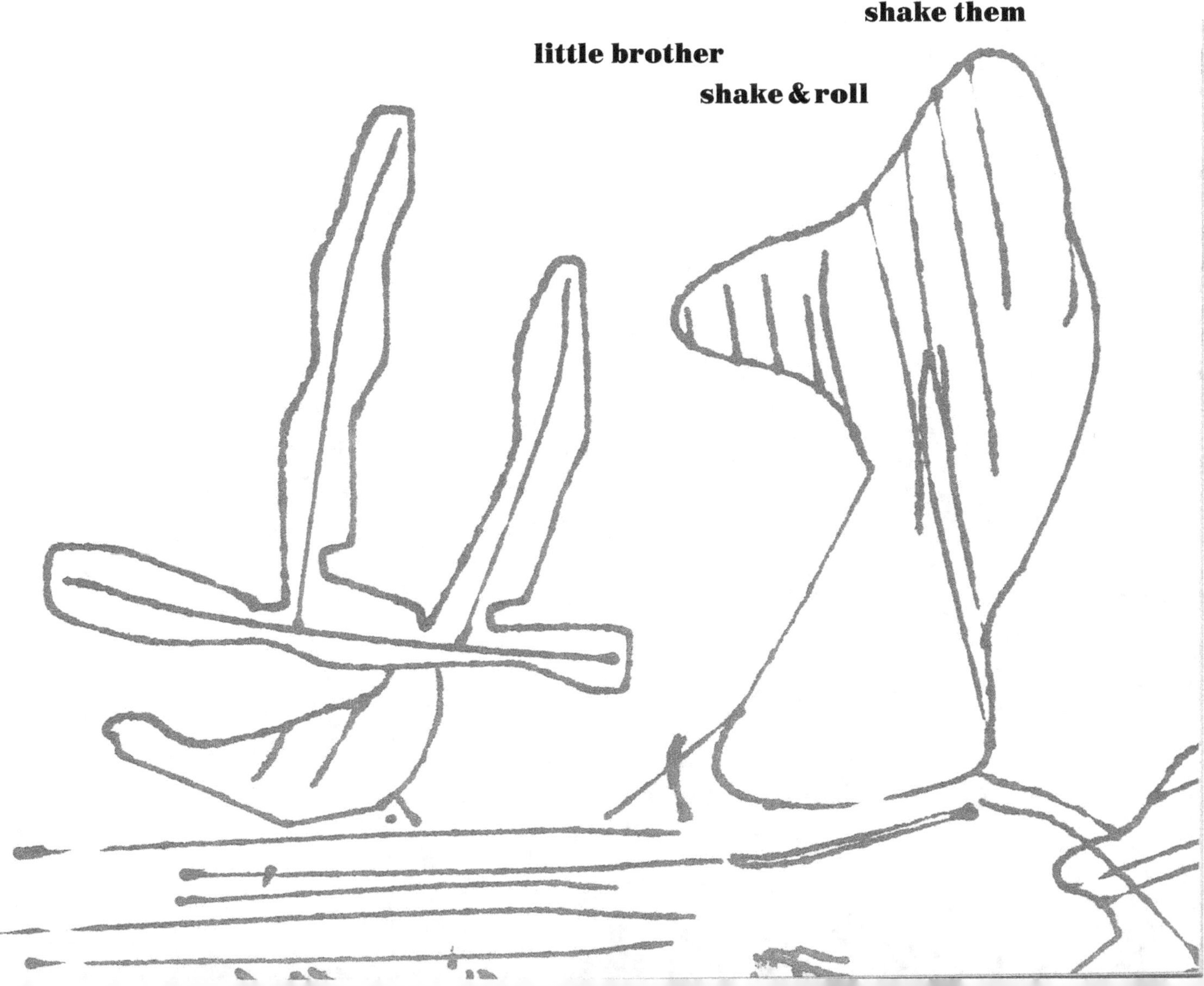

six

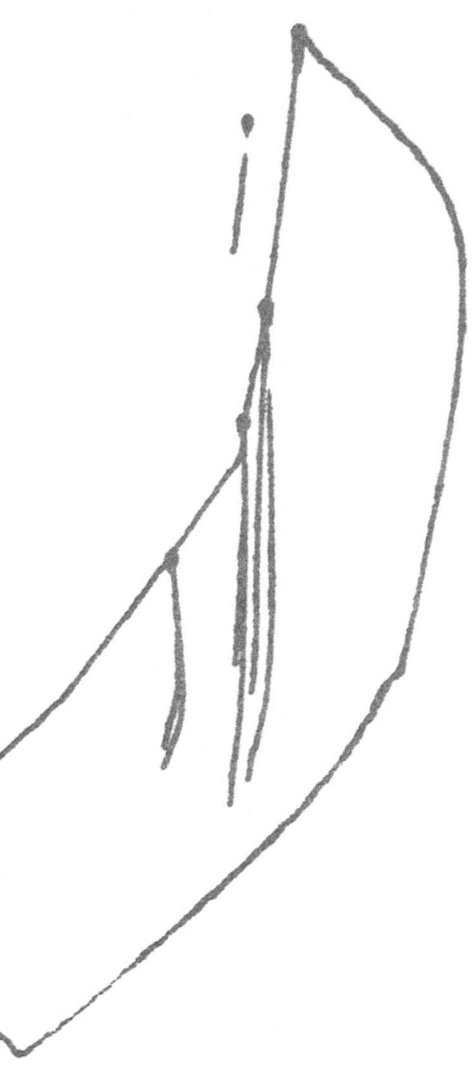

in one tree
one stick
who makes the sound of cracking
cracking wood?
in one tree
one stick
who makes the sound of cracking
cracking wood?
there in the flower world
the tree world
you do not have my
long grey body
in one tree
one stick
who makes the sound of cracking
cracking wood?

seven

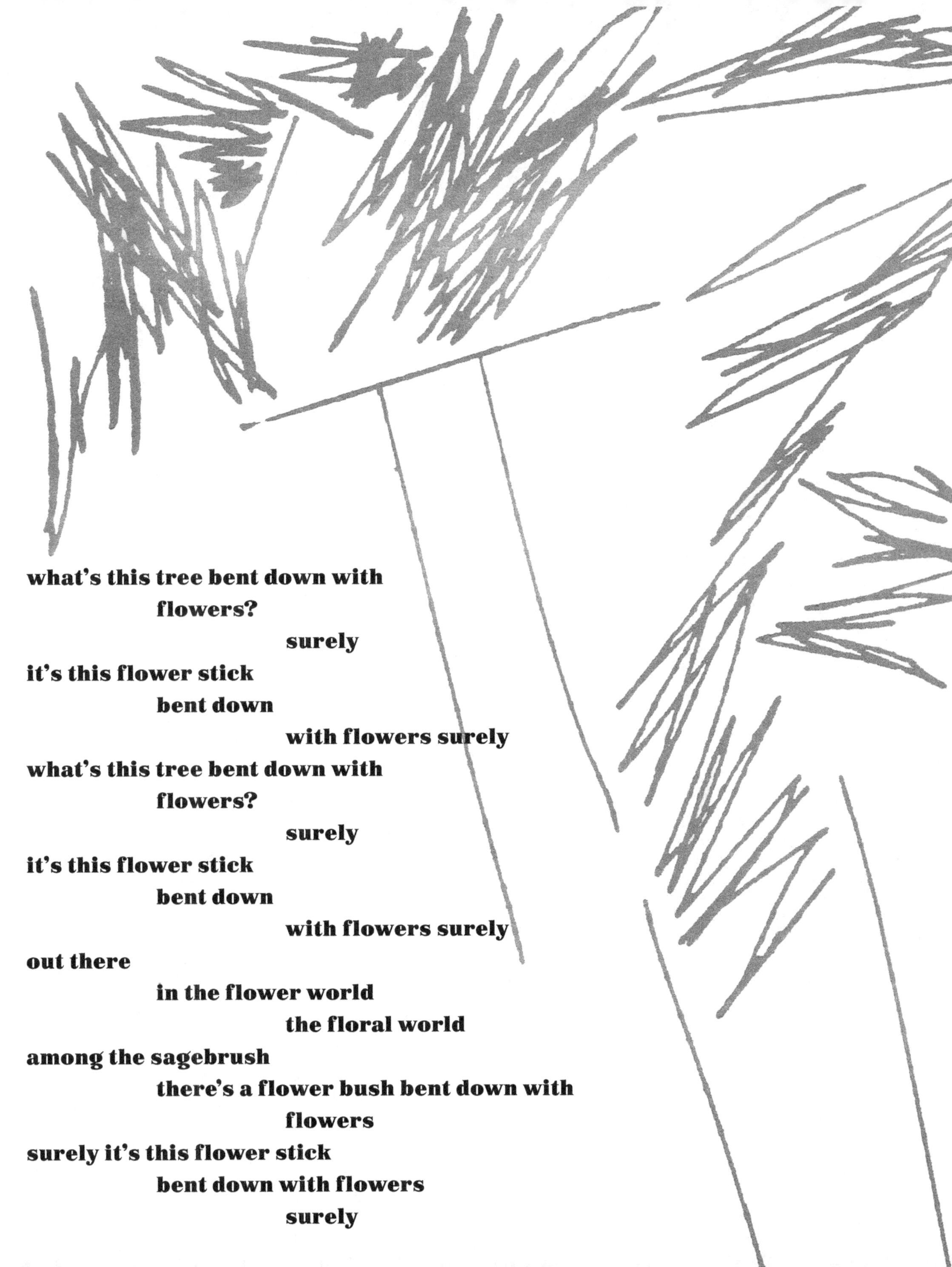

what's this tree bent down with
        flowers?
                surely
it's this flower stick
        bent down
                with flowers surely
what's this tree bent down with
        flowers?
                surely
it's this flower stick
        bent down
                with flowers surely
out there
        in the flower world
                the floral world
among the sagebrush
        there's a flower bush bent down with
                flowers
surely it's this flower stick
        bent down with flowers
                surely

eight

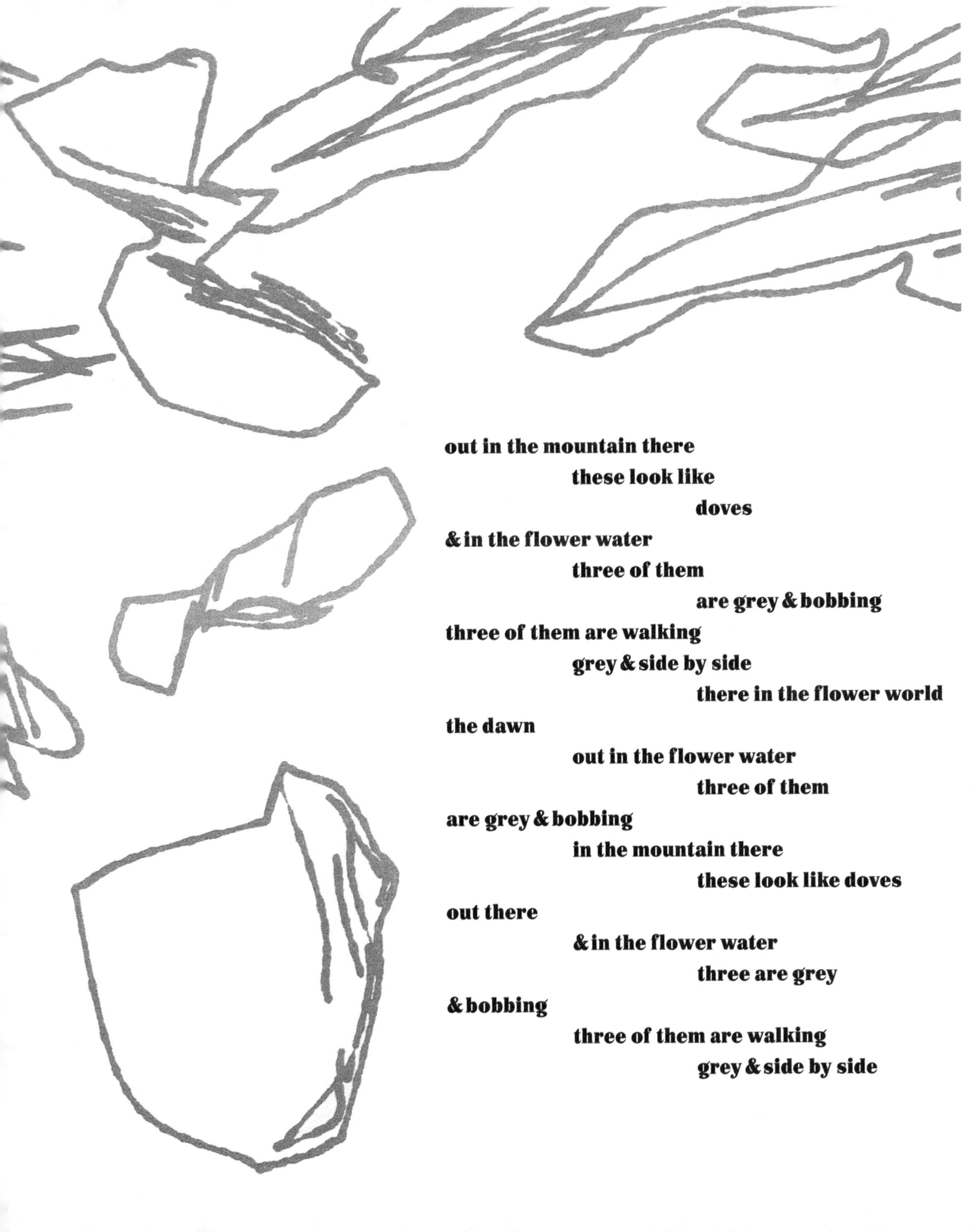
out in the mountain there
these look like
doves
& in the flower water
three of them
are grey & bobbing
three of them are walking
grey & side by side
there in the flower world
the dawn
out in the flower water
three of them
are grey & bobbing
in the mountain there
these look like doves
out there
& in the flower water
three are grey
& bobbing
three of them are walking
grey & side by side

nine

you
          like a mountain squirrel
                    old enchanter
sounding large
          & like a mountain squirrel
                    old enchanter
sounding large
          & like a mountain squirrel
                    old enchanter
there in the flower world
          the dawn
                    there in its light
that big place over there
          that mountain canyon
                    sounding large
& like a mountain squirrel
          old enchanter
                    sounding large

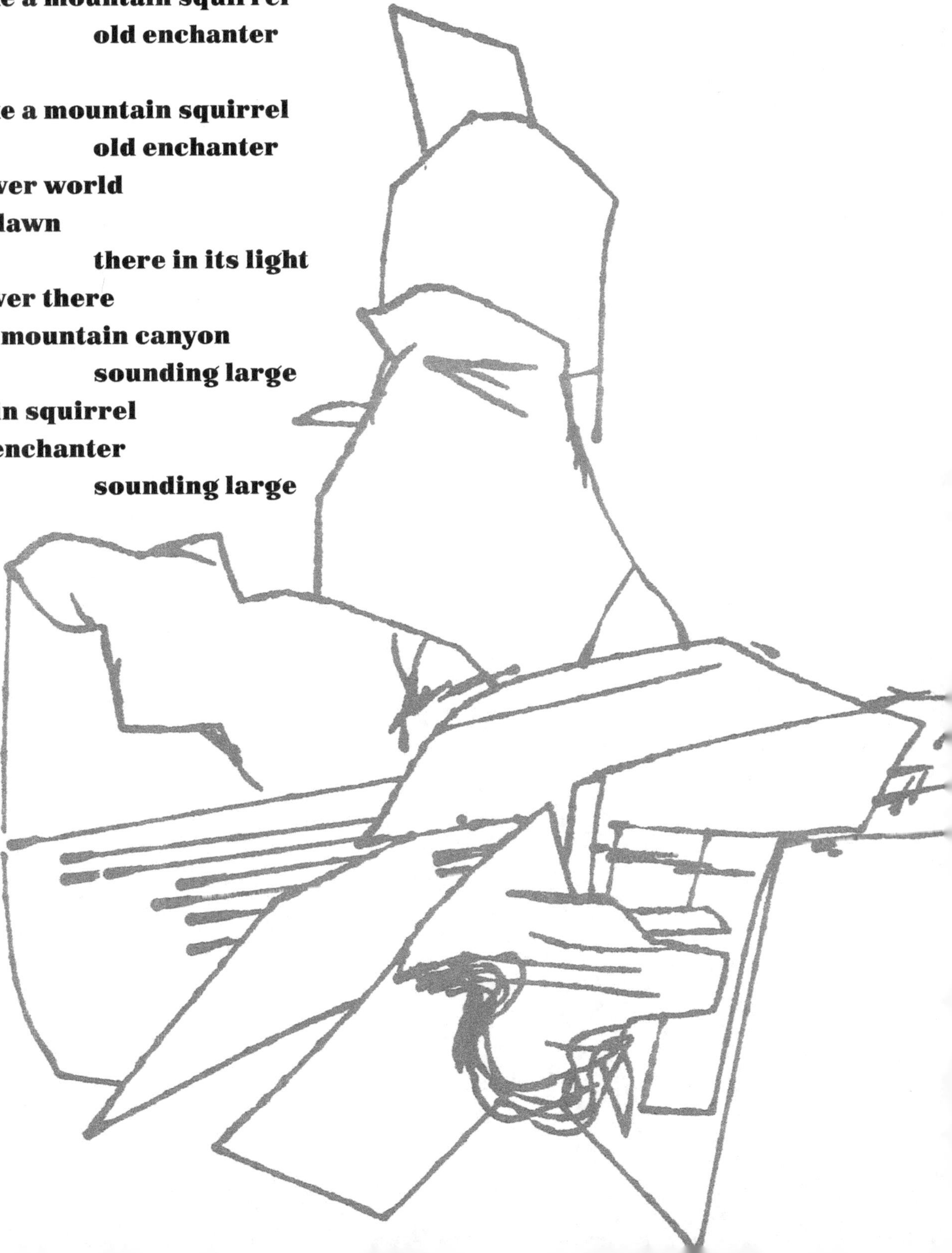

ten

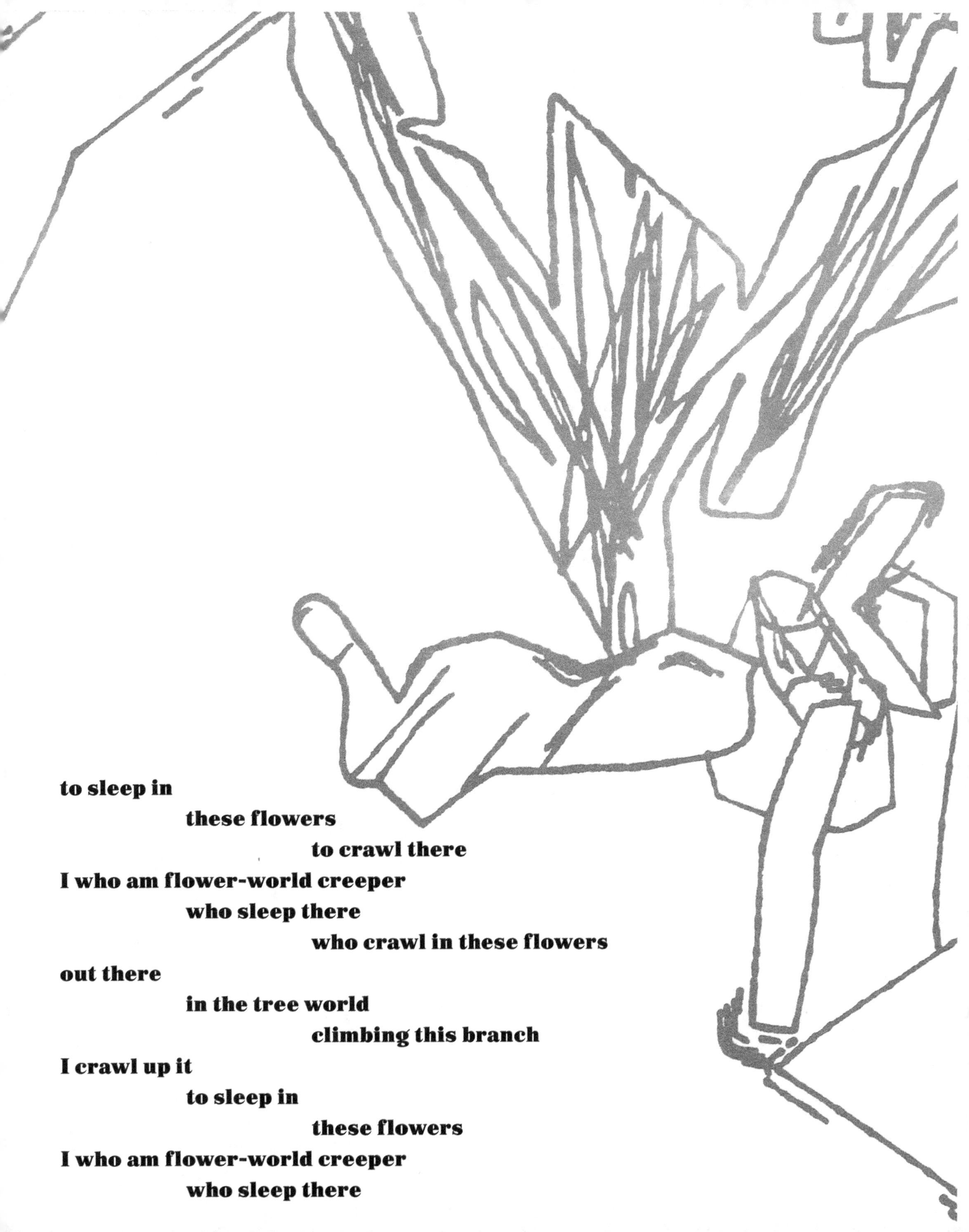

to sleep in

      these flowers

         to crawl there

I who am flower-world creeper

      who sleep there

         who crawl in these flowers

out there

      in the tree world

         climbing this branch

I crawl up it

      to sleep in

         these flowers

I who am flower-world creeper

      who sleep there

eleven

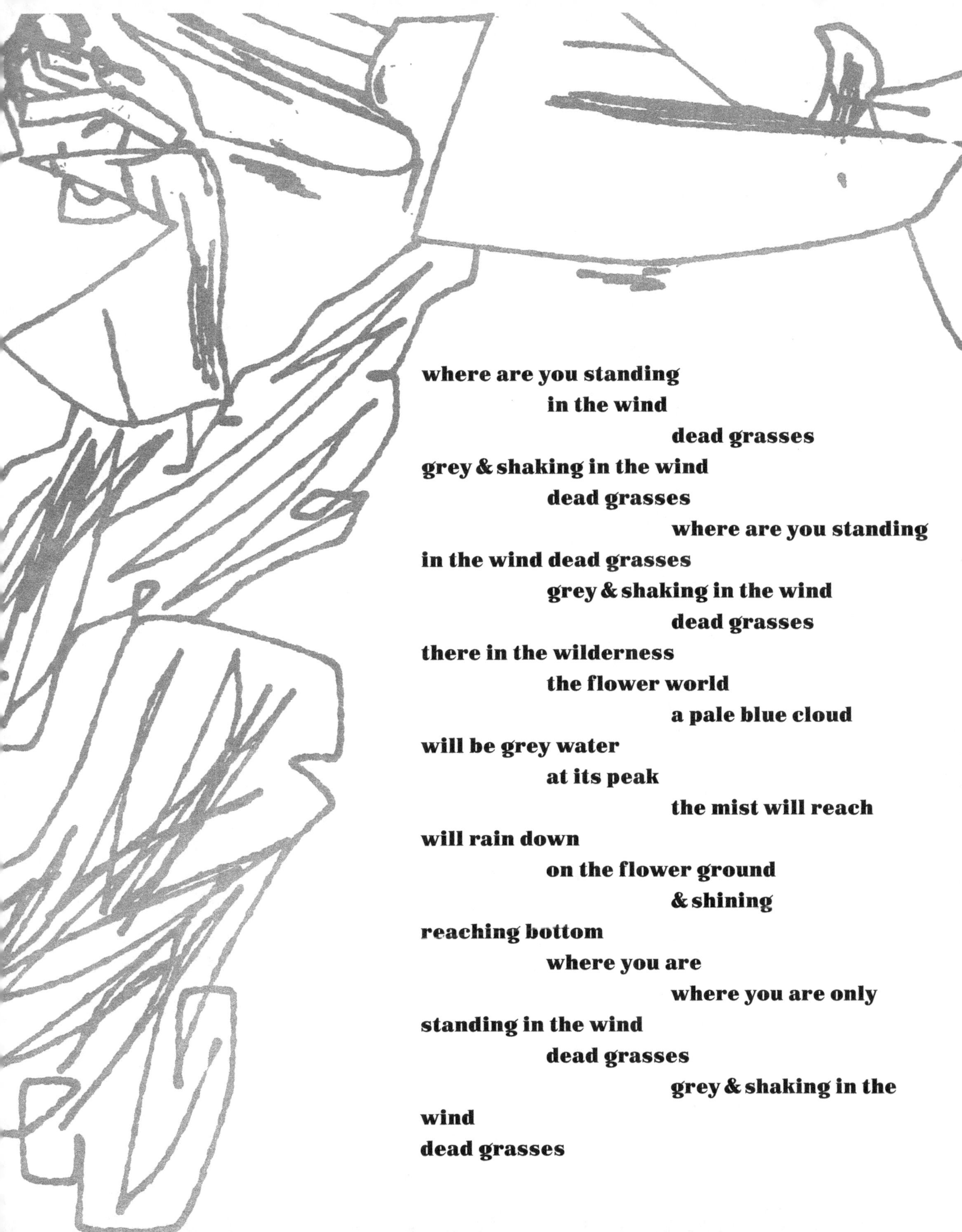

where are you standing
in the wind
dead grasses
grey & shaking in the wind
dead grasses
where are you standing
in the wind dead grasses
grey & shaking in the wind
dead grasses
there in the wilderness
the flower world
a pale blue cloud
will be grey water
at its peak
the mist will reach
will rain down
on the flower ground
& shining
reaching bottom
where you are
where you are only
standing in the wind
dead grasses
grey & shaking in the
wind
dead grasses

twelve

ah brother
        they want us to kill
                this beaver
they want us to kill
        ah brother
                this beaver
this beaver
        ah brother
                they want us to kill
with a bow & arrow
        they want us to kill it
                ah brother
with hair standing up
        this were waiting
                & ran from us
broke down their doors to get in
        now they want us
                to kill it
ah brother
        with a bow & arrow
                ah brother
they want us to kill it

thirteen

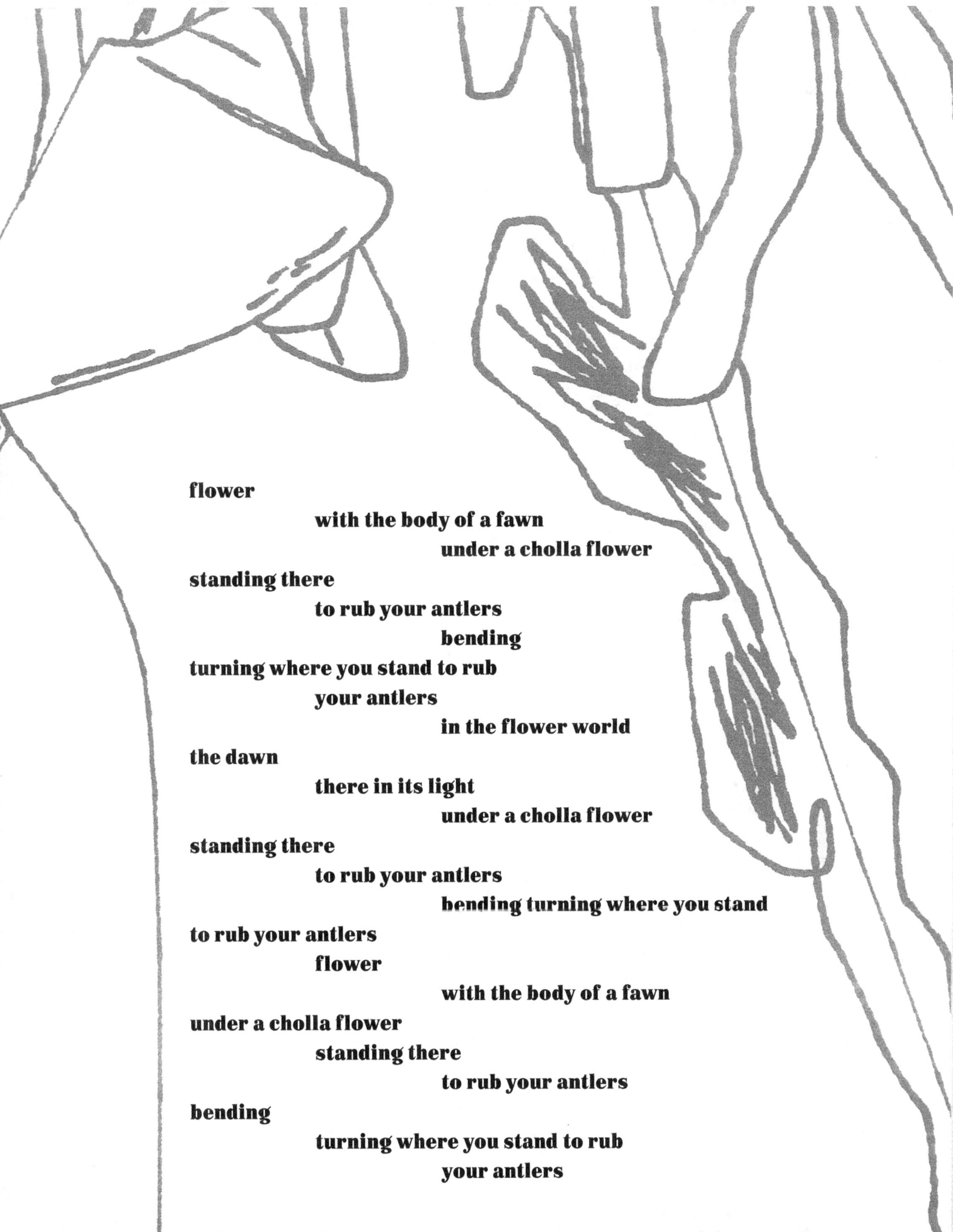

flower
   with the body of a fawn
      under a cholla flower
standing there
   to rub your antlers
      bending
turning where you stand to rub
   your antlers
      in the flower world
the dawn
   there in its light
      under a cholla flower
standing there
   to rub your antlers
      bending turning where you stand
to rub your antlers
   flower
      with the body of a fawn
under a cholla flower
   standing there
      to rub your antlers
bending
   turning where you stand to rub
      your antlers

fourteen

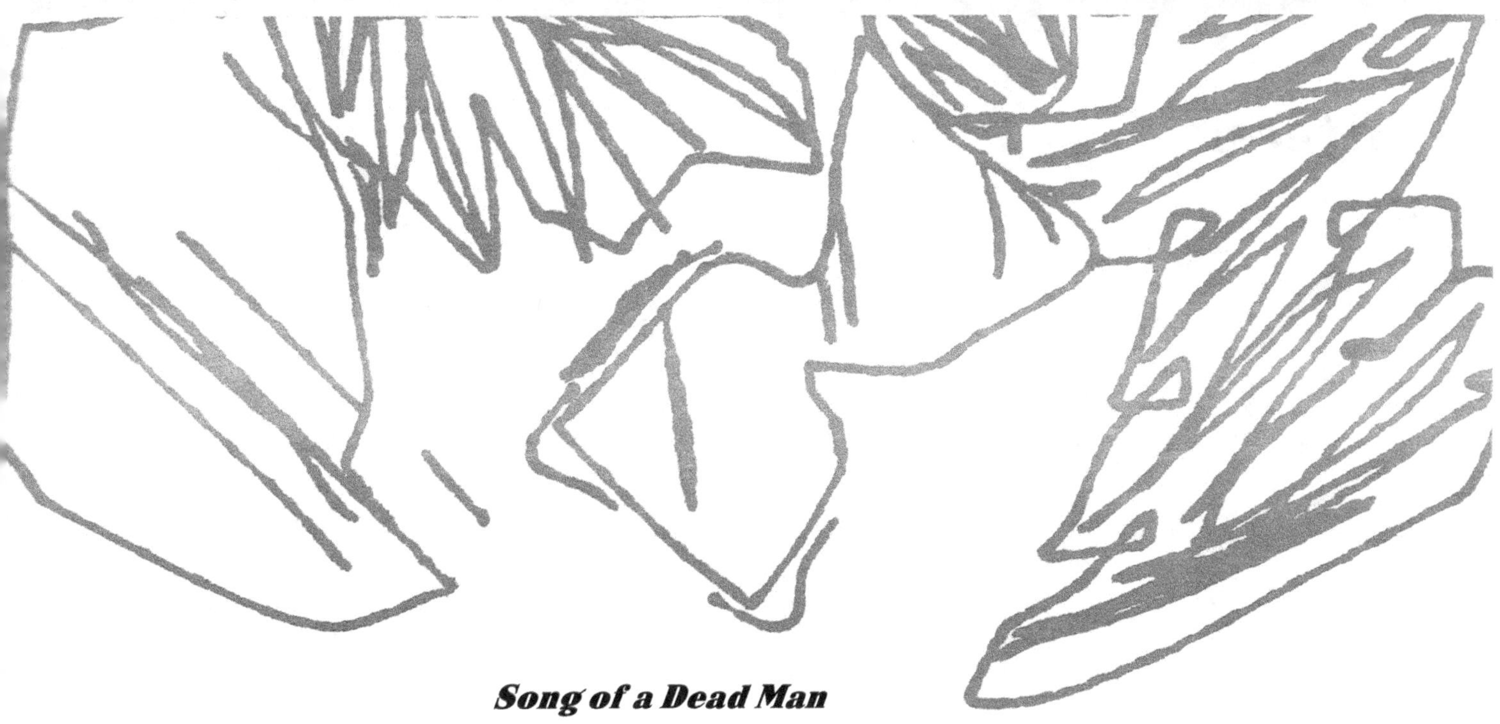

Song of a Dead Man

I do not want these flowers
      moving
            but the flowers
want to move
      I do not want these flowers
            moving
but the flowers
      want to move
            I do not want these flowers
moving
      but the flowers
            want to move
out in the flower world
      the dawn
            over a road of flowers
I do not want these flowers
      moving
            but the flowers
want to move
      I do not want these flowers
            moving
but the flowers
      the flowers
            want to move

fifteen

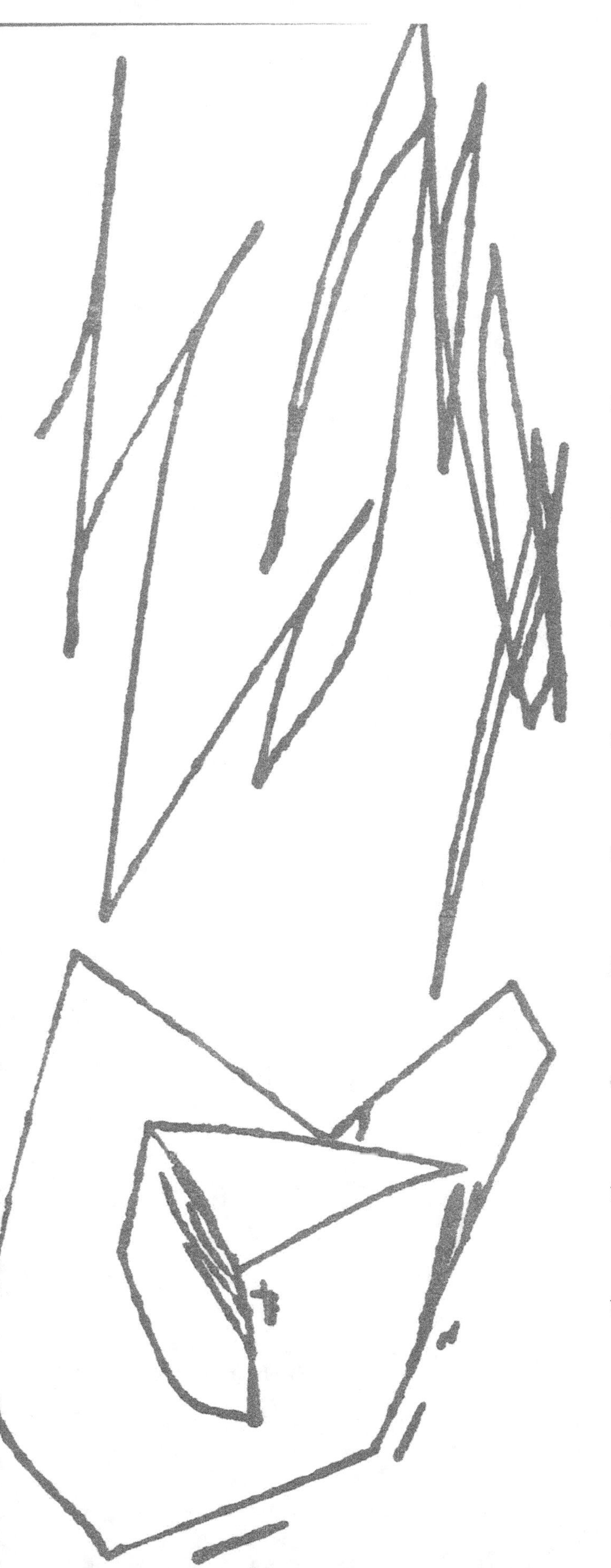

now the cloud
      will break
            the cloud will break
& now
      the cloud will break
         the cloud
will break
      & now the cloud
        will break
the cloud will break
      there in the flower world
        under the dawn
this pale blue cloud
      will be grey water
        at its peak
the mist will reach
      will rain down
        shining
& reaching bottom
      now the cloud
        will break
the cloud will break
      & now
          the cloud will break
the cloud
      will break

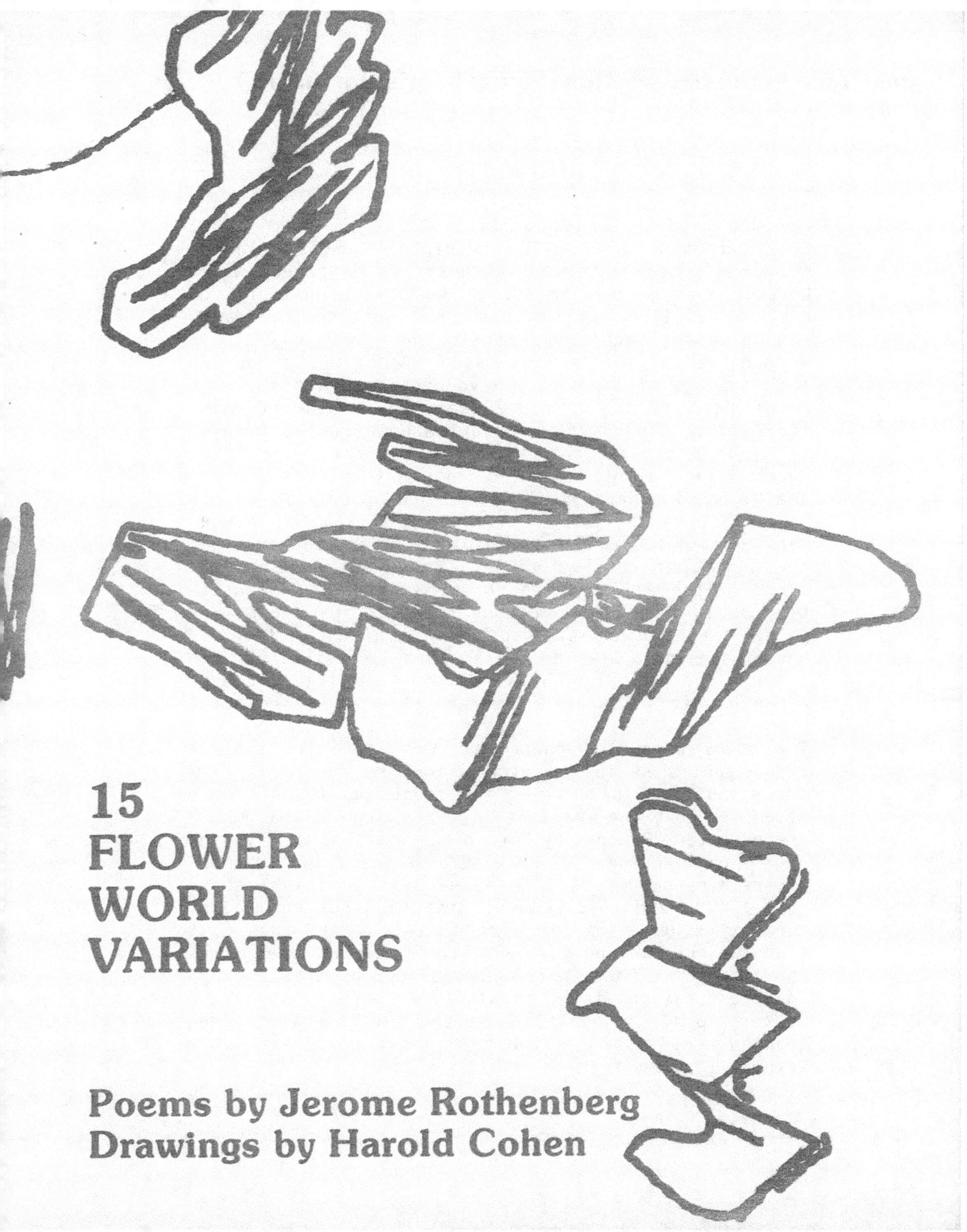

15 FLOWER WORLD VARIATIONS

Poems by Jerome Rothenberg
Drawings by Harold Cohen

post-face to the 15 variations (from original printing)

For the last three years (81/82/83) I was witness to
Deer Dances at New Pascua Pueblo in Tuscon, Arizona
-- not a spooky other-worldliness, as Castaneda would
have it, but the enactment, through religion & art, of
high & brilliant worlds one step outside-the-human.
For these the Yaquis have their own names: huya aniya
= enchanted world; or seyawailo = flower world; or, in
the language of some of the younger inheritors, "wil-
derness" as such. The dance (set against the parodis-
tic Pascola Clowns as alternative flower world beings)
is tight & classical & contained (always) within the
narrow space alloted to the dancer. (Constrast, e.g.,
the Nijinskian capers of the trumped-up Deer Dancer in
Mexico's urban Ballet Folkloricao, etc.) It is a won-
der to see & to dream back into one's own language. But
the dance, of course, has its language as well, the
words of the accompanying songs; & these, as transla-
tion opens them to us, become the principle means for
bringing that flower world to life. The process, then, is
one of singing & stating, re-singing & re-stating, into
a new wilderness "in which," as our old friend George
Oppen has it, "the wild deer/startle, and stare out."

The poems presented haere are from literal transla-
tions published in Carleton Wilder's *The Yaqui Deer
Dance* (1963). I have taken the images as found & have
attempted to bring them (again) into song. (The comput-
er-generated drawings by Harold Cohen act as well as the
most direct analogues I know to a sense of those human/
other-than-human worlds from which the original songs
come.) I have no desire otherwise to argue the poems'
veracity (they seem to me no further "off" than most
translations) beyond the question of whether they allow
the image of a flower world to come out in the reading.
The presentation, then, is simply as poems that do the
work (or play) of poetry -- in the belief that the en-
chanted world is there and here, as a possession that
we hold in common.

JEROME ROTHENBERG

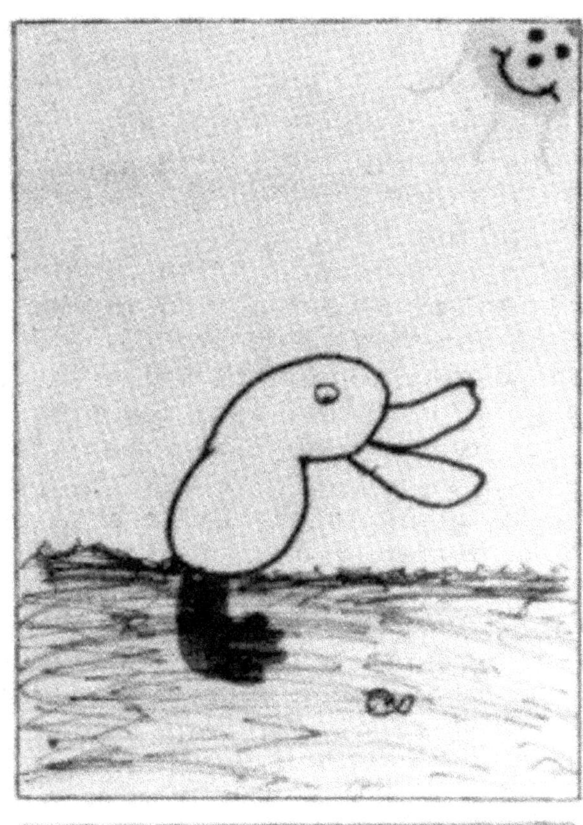

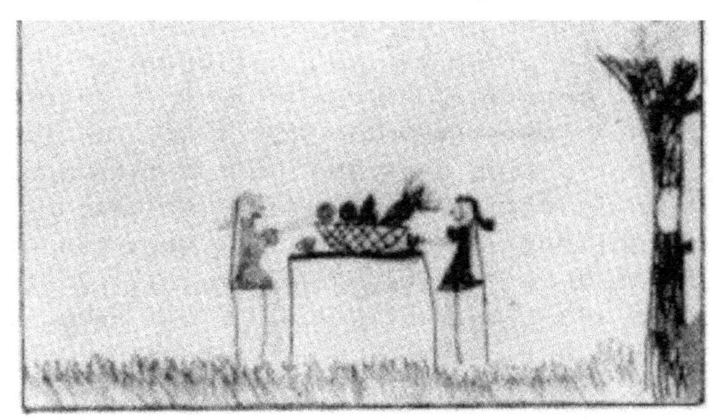

fig 2   fig 1

fig 3   fig 4

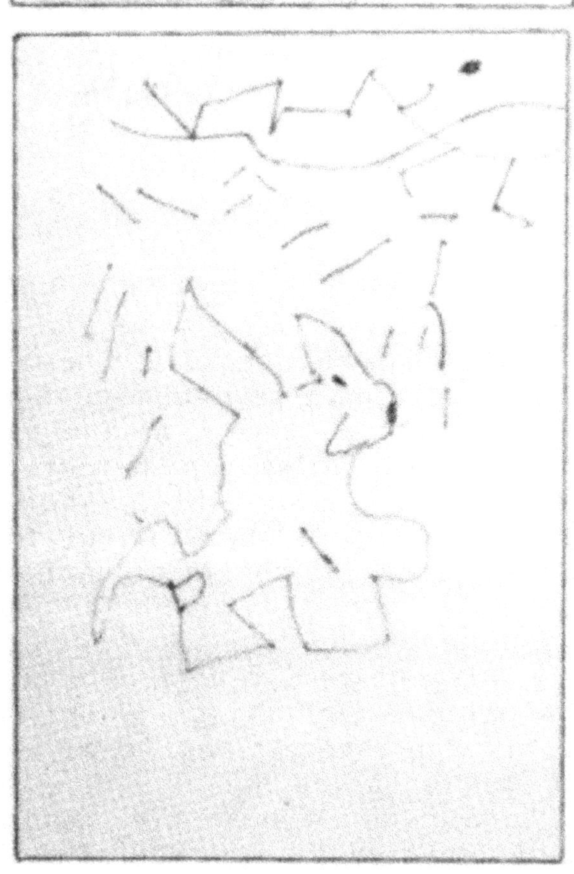

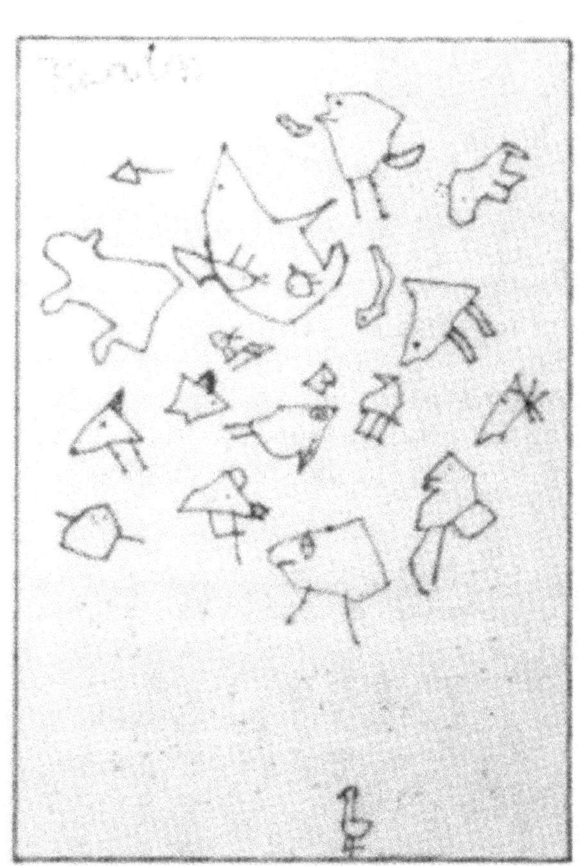

The students there were up to forty years older than Karin and Sherry, and their habitual modes involved different conventions to those of the children; but they were cer- tainly no less conventional.)

But the more immediately noticeable differences between the two modes relate less to the formal aspects of the drawings than to the level of imagination and inventiveness wich Sherry and Karin exercise in making them. When Karin decides to sign her name in a manner appropriate to the game (4), she is mak- ing a witty comment about the nature of drawing at a level of insightfulness we might not expect from a seven year-old. If we compare the bird in one of her dot-drawings (5) with the drawing of a duck made just half an hour earli- er, we are struck by the fact that she is evi- dently capable of rather acute observation, although it required the setting up of unfamiliar, and presum- ably chal- lenging, circumstances to allow her to exercise that capability.

What becomes clear, in fact, is that there is a significant difference be- tween an image of a bird, and an image of an image of a bird. The earli- er drawing is less a duck than it is a toy duck, less the result of ob- serving what the real world is like than it is the result of learning what draw- ings — of the world — are supposed to look like. It is conventional in the precise sense that its conventions are the common property of that sub-culture we call children, where their stability is maintained both by the children's desire to conform and by the adult desire that they should.

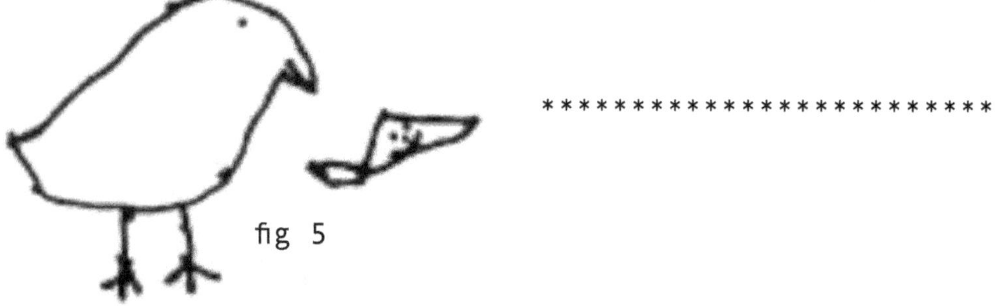

fig 5

* *

I incline strongly to the view that we all spend our lives -- not merely our childhood -- trying to effect an accept- able and workable compromise between the internal demands for the satisfaction of our individual psychic needs, and the demands made upon us by the culture within which we live, for the sake of the stability, if not necessarily the ultimate well-being, of the culture itself. This is not to say that the things we do, like drawings, singing, talking, do not grow from the most fundamental patterns of the mind but that the cultural rules imposed for their exercise may lead to behavioral patterns quite at variance with these deeper ones.

Most children are able to build their early images without difficulty with marks which result directly from simple physical movements, just as the Af- rican sculptor has no difficulty satisfying his representational needs with conceptually simple forms requiring simple manufacturing skills (6). The notion of representation which held sway in Europe for nearly five hundred years, on the other hand, requires the student to spend a minimum of three years persuading his eye to see what it is supposed to see, and disciplining his hand to move as it is supposed to move. These movements are arbitrary with respect to the individual, since they have to be determined by events in the world — the random play of light and shade on objects -- which have nothing to do with the way his shoulder and wrist are articulated. The reconciliation which the artist in this tradition is obliged to make is a striking example of the sort of compromise I am referring to.

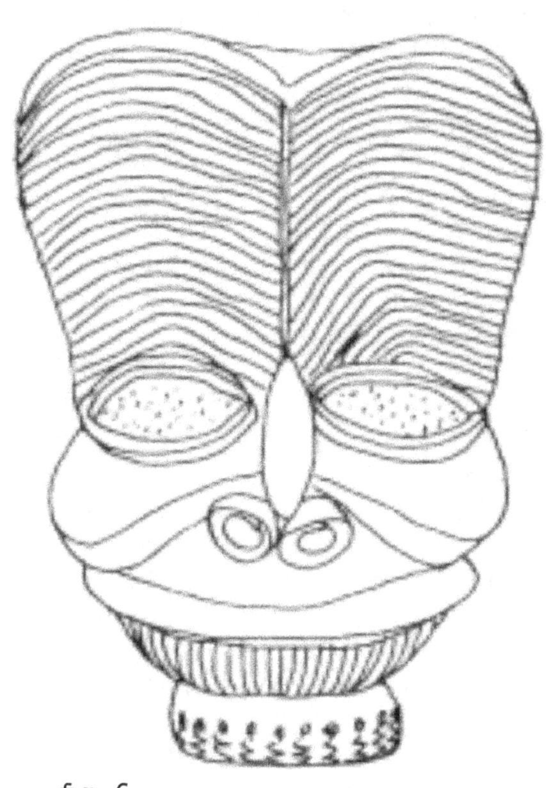

fig 6

We do not pay for our membership of the culture on a one-day-on, one-day-off basis. All our behavior is acculturat- ed to some degree, and any attempt to isolate a discreet behavioral mode which we might think of as "natural" would be fruitless. Yet we might still find in the underlying structures of behavior aspects which are evidently not fashioned by the constraints of any particular culture, and this would be as close as we might come to a notion of "naturalness". It will be the tracking down of these as- pects with which I will be concerned, knowing very well that their separation from other aspects is a theoretical one.

Much of our mental activity seems to involve complex schema of entities standing for other entities, and we would prob- ably agree that the externalizing and manipulation of images, as such, grows directly from basic mind functions. But that area of symbol-manipulation which is directed towards communication between individuals and between groups must obviously involve highly acculturated perfor- mance. For a symbolic structure to stand any reasonable chance of being unambiguously understood, its maker must both have clear knowledge of the expectations which the reader will bring to its reading, and be prepared to accept the constraints imposed by those expectations. Communica- tion is possible within a culture only because of existing agreements as to what entity is to stand for what entity, and how it is to be presented to be recognized as doing so. At an even more basic level, this implies also that all the involved parties know about the same entities: which may be true, more or less, within the same culture, but is unlikely to be true from one culture to another.

These would seem not to be very promising conditions for the exercise of imagination, inventiveness, and all those other virtues we associate with the making of art, or, indeed, for our understanding of art produced by any cul- ture other than our own. But I think we have to conclude that art never has been devoted primarily to the cultural function of communication, and in- deed it may never have been thought that it did before our own time. The more his- toric view within our own culture pictures the artist in communion with variously-conceived extra-human sources of inspiration and wisdom, explicitly acknowledging the fact that if he speaks on behalf of the community, he does not speak with its voice or in terms which will necessarily be understood.

Art history deals with the problem of tracking and identi- fying the transformations which continuously modify the significance of symbols within the changing cultural con- tinuum. But there are other problems of a more fundamental kind which fall outside the scope of orthodox iconology. Any art theory which begins with a view of the artist as serving primarily the cultural need to formulate and transmit explicit meanings inevitably ends up viewing the whole system as a sort of noisy telephone network, in which the receiver strives constantly to reconstruct the original message. Yet the cultural mismatch between artist and viewer must then be a major source of noise in the system, and we account for the discrepancies between what the ar- tist "has in mind" and what the viewer thinks he under- stands, by the notion of "interpretation". We do not necessarily have any evidence beyond our own "interpretations", however, as to what, if anything, the artist had in mind in the first place.

This emphasis upon the specifically cultural use of symbols has left us without any account of the underlying struc- tures of image-generating behavior more convincing than the Divine Muse, and some contemporary variant of that theme usually passes for explanation. I am always a little shocked to recall that it is only about fifty years since Paul Klee declared that it is a sin against the Creative Spirit for the artist to work when not inspired. After nearly thirty years spent in making art, in the company of other artists, I am prepared to declare that the artist has no hot-line to the infinite, and no uniquely delineated mind functions. What he does, he does with the same general-purpose equipment that everybody has, and if his use of it is in any respect unusual, that very fact points to the need for a model of image-generating behavior which concentrates specifically upon behavioral mechanisms rather than upon products.

In particular, I believe we will need to adopt a view of the artist as indulging in the generation of what I will call image-rich material as a self-satisfying procedure primarily, and only secondarily involved in the manipula- tion of culturally stabilized symbols: performing that secondary function, moreover, in a manner more in keeping with the essentially self-seeking character of the primary one.

****

You will see that I am back to the fundamental dichotomy between the internal psychic, and the external cultural determinants to an individual's behavior. The two are not available for examination in isolation of each other, for the rather obvious reason that human beings live in cul- tures. As far as image-generating behavior is concerned, however, it seems reasonable to speculate that image-rich material arises from the innately human domain, for the reason that the cultural determinants which act upon the individual tend, by definition, towards conventionalizing; towards the rigid binding of symbol to stabilized meaning. To reflect broader experience more accurately, we have to look, not for symbols which are unambiguously understood within their own culture — however powerfully they may function there — but for material which can flow between cultures, and which is constantly re-used to mesh with new and diverse meanings as it does so. What we think of as our culture is no more than a moment in time, a cross-section of a continuum. All but an infinitesimally small part of all the symbols and symbol-potent material which reaches us comes to us from other points in time and from other more or less remote cultural states.

In some cases, what we find ourselves responding to comes from cultures so remote that we simply have to acknowledge that we cannot possibly know what its original significance was. I am thinking particularly of the petroglyphs which are to be found throughout Nevada and California (7). We know nothing to speak of concerning the people who made them or what they made them for, or even how long ago they were made. We cannot seriously pretend even to misunder- stand their original significance, and what speculation exists is based upon evidence quite extrinsic to the marks themselves. Yet the generations of anthropologists who have added their speculations to an increasing but unrevealing literature bear witness to the power of the glyphs: the power, not to communicate explicit meanings within the cul- ture within which they arose, but to trigger and direct our own innate propensities for attaching significance to events.

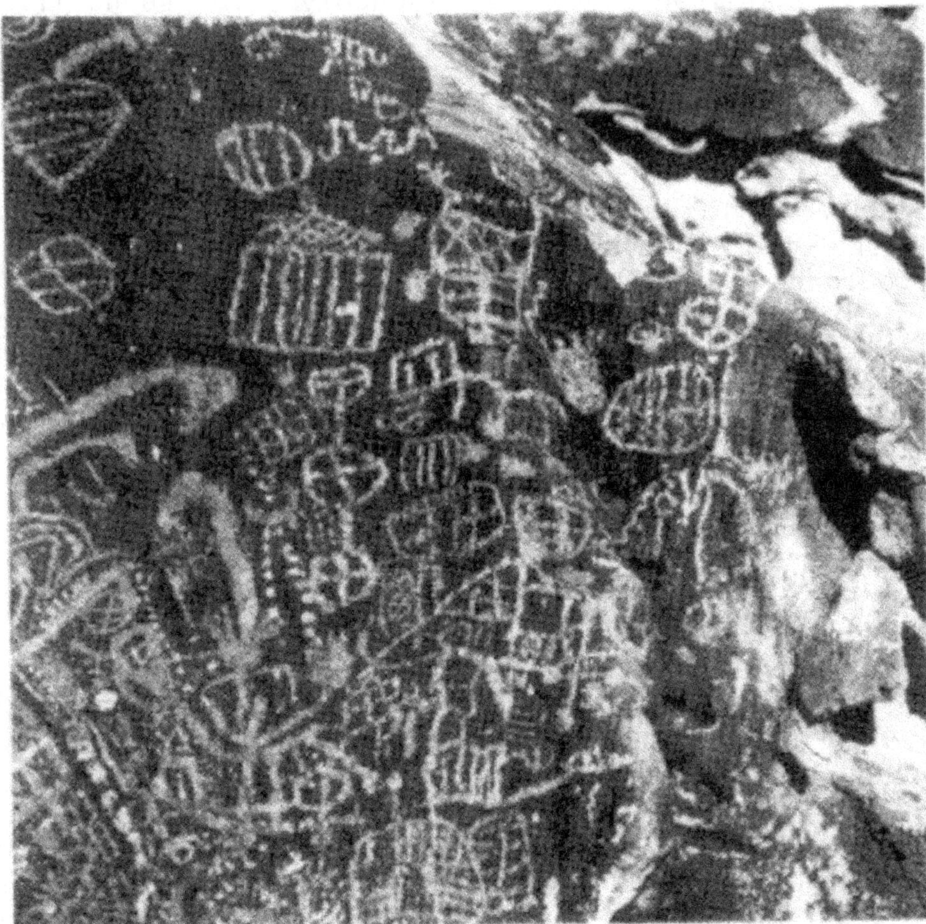

fig 7

To account for the pressure which these marks are capable of exerting over so total a cultural void, would we not have to assume that their power derives from the essentially human determinants to their making? that it reflects patterns of behavior so deep-rooted in the human organism as to be considered as constant for all human beings regardless of their particular patterns of acculturation?

The question would be entirely speculative, not to say gratuitous, if we could proceed only by the analysis of existing examples, for the reason that what is present for analysis is the object, not the behavior which generated it. Any plausible conclusion would be exactly as good as any other plausible conclusion in the absence of any possible verification.

I will not claim that my own work offers definitive verification of any conclusion, but I will claim it as an attempt, at least, to deal with behavior rather than with objects. Analysis of a range of objects, from the Californian petroglyphs at one extreme to my own drawing at the other, has served mainly to suggest a sort of minimum configuration of deep-level behavioral mechanisms, which have then been used as the basis of a computer program capable of generating and dealing with graphic material.

In other words, the choice of mechanisms was largely intui- tive and arbitrary. I suspected that I would be on reasonably safe ground if I limited myself, at the outset at least, to what I assumed to be perceptual primitives, and I selected three: the ability to differentiate between figure and ground, to differentiate between open forms and closed forms, and to differentiate between insideness and outsideness.

Since the choice was arbitrary, I did not think it needed further justification at that stage of a questionable undertaking. Yet I thought that actually justification could be found: both in the fact that young children evidently differentiate between closed forms like circles and trian- gles, and open forms like crosses, well before they are able to differentiate between circles and triangles: and also because of the persistence, throughout the long human history of mark-making, of motifs like mazes. It seemed to me that much of what we grace with the name "primitive" actually demonstrates a sophisticated awareness of the nature of the perceptual open/closed duality, for the fas- cination of the maze — the image, I mean, rather than the physical maze — must surely rest on the difficulty of knowing at a single glance whether it is open or closed.

The point of the strategy — the building of a computer program — was not to see whether the presence of these behavioral primitives would add a sense of authenticity to the output. It was to see whether the program could gen- erate image-rich material In a controlled context where it would be clear that the effect was not the result of some- thing else. That would certainly not have been the case if I had tried to limit myself to any particular set of behavioral primitives, and I have taken some care to see that I do not influence the running of the program. As it has been designed, it operates without any human assistance or intervention. There is no way to interfere with it while it is running, and no convenient way to change its parame- ters before the start of any drawing.

Much more important, it has no data at its disposal: no lexicon of previous- ly-described forms which it could pull out, run through a variety of transfor- mations, and assemble into a picture. As a matter of fact, it has no trans- formations available to it, either.

An argument could be made, of course, that the whole program constitutes a process description of its output, although it would then have to be seen as the description common to an endless array of different drawings, since the program never produces the same drawing twice. But the sig- nificance of the lack of data is a more complex one. There is no difficulty about writing a com- puter program which generates drawings endlessly, depending at least upon what "different" is understood to mean. Here the question was whether the degree and kind of differentness would correspond to the variety we might expect from a human image-maker. Would the individual drawings, generated in the absence of any knowledge of the world and its objects, nevertheless function as though they were made by a human image-maker, in the sense that they might appear to be making reference to the world and its objects?

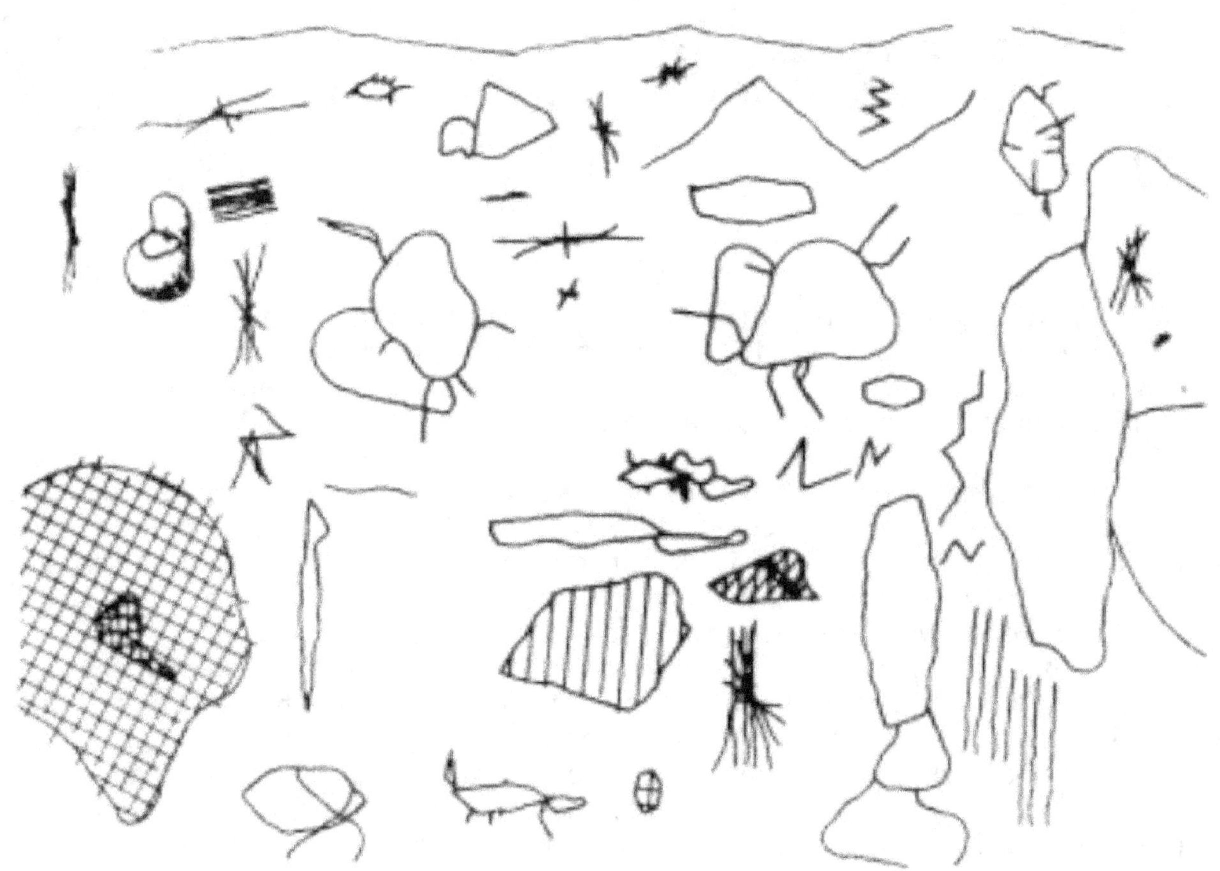

fig 8

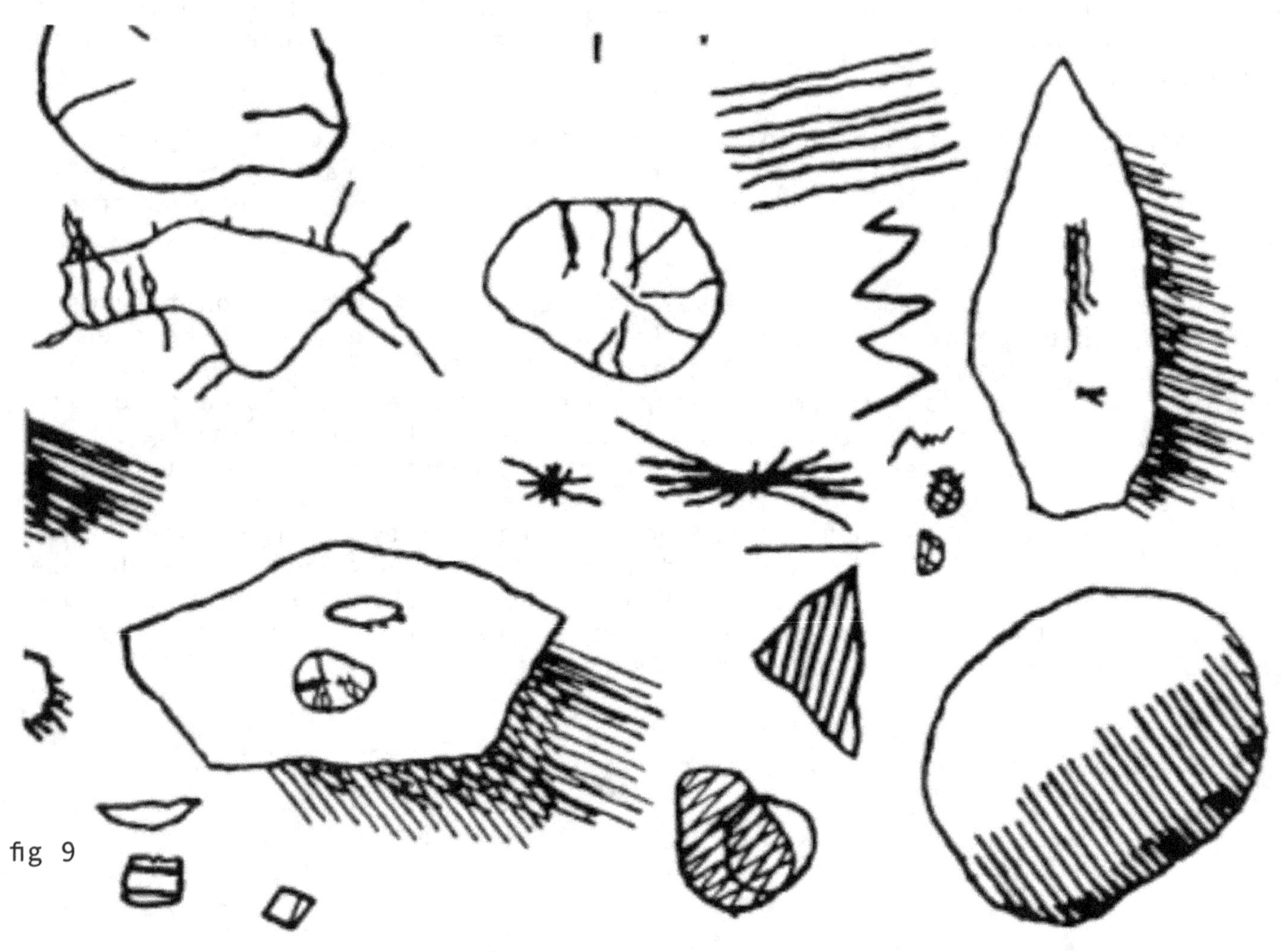

The answer seems to be affirmative, at least to the degree that most people evidently have some difficulty in believing that the drawings (8-10) were not made by a human artist: an artist, moreover, with a distinct sense of humor and a marked tendency towards narrative.

As the prime mover of these drawings — I still have some difficulty regarding myself as their maker in any conventional sense — I find myself in a curious position involving a not-too-serious parody on the notion of divine in- spira- tion. It takes about two weeks after seeing one of the drawings for the first time for me to lose my awareness of it as machine output. I can hardly regard it as my own, because I have no recollection of having participated physically in its making, and it seems to have come to me from another time and place. We might see this as a comment on the persistence of myths, perhaps. But if romance dies hard, the facts are left to be accounted for. If we find elements in these drawings reminiscent of African masks and comets, figures suggestive of turtles and submarines (10), it is a fact that the elements and figures which evoke those objects were made by the program. It is also a fact that the program knows nothing of African masks, comets, turtles or submarines.

Explaining how these effects come about in the absence of any specific inten-
tionality is difficult, primarily because they cannot be identified with the
action of individual parts of the program. There is, I mean, nothing like a
sub- marine subroutine. In form, the program is a productionsystem; and, like
other such systems, this one accomplishes two things. It describes the condi-
tions which may arise in the world of the program — in this case the developing
drawing — and it lists the acceptable responses to partic- ular combinations
of these conditions.

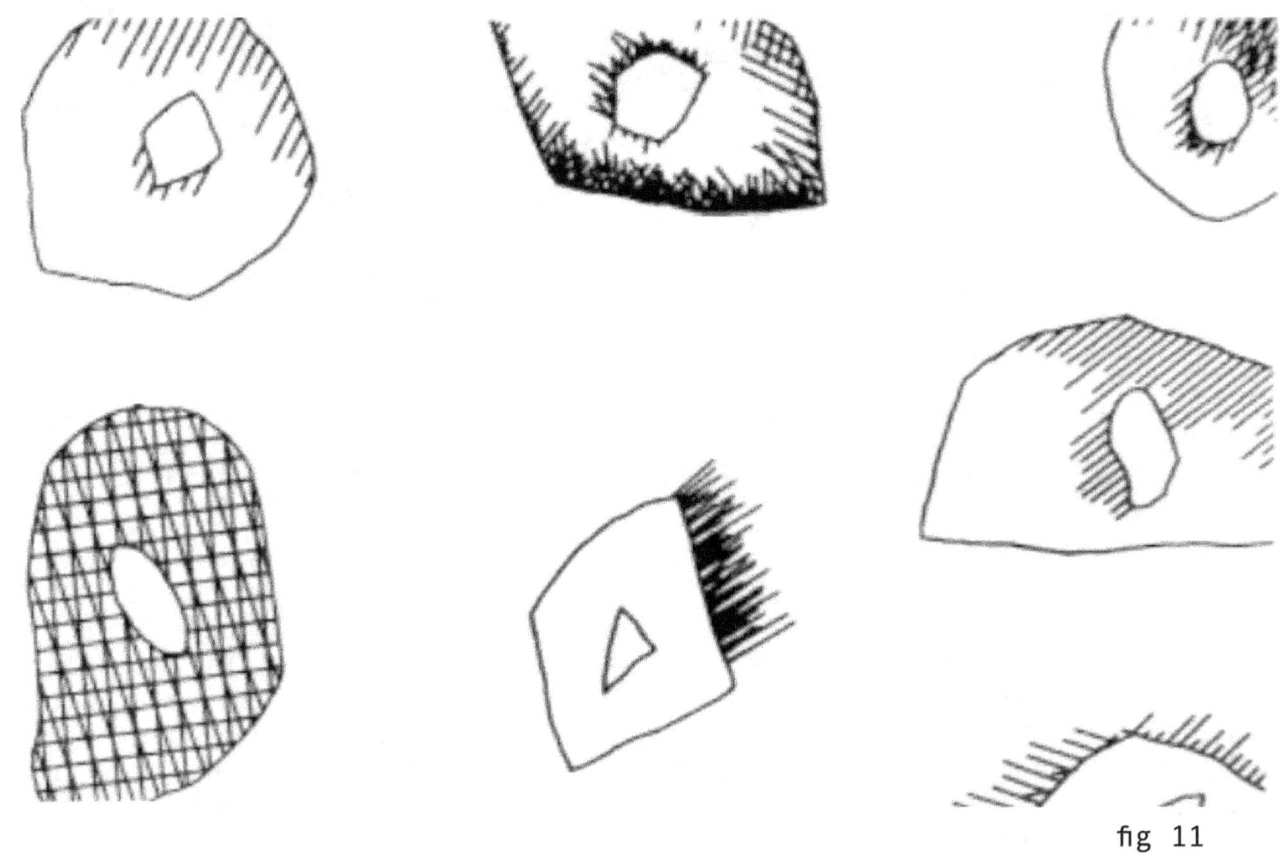

fig 11

The left part of a production tests for the patterns, the particular combina-
tions of conditions which characterize the state of the world at any moment.
The right part of a production changes the state of the world, since all the
acceptable responses act upon the world directly or indirectly. The new com-
binations of conditions will then be trapped by other productions; and the
process continues, in this event-driven fashion, from the initial empty state
until one of several world states elicits the response that the drawing is
done.

The left part of a production is able to recognize that a form is closed rather
than open, just as the right part is able to produce a closed form, or effect
closure upon an open one. A complete production might recognize that part of
the field of the drawing is occupied by a closed form with another closed form
inside it; and that it is surrounded by similar closed forms, all of which have
been shaded in one way or another (11). And it might respond — for example —
by shading the figure, leaving the inner one as a hole in the middle.

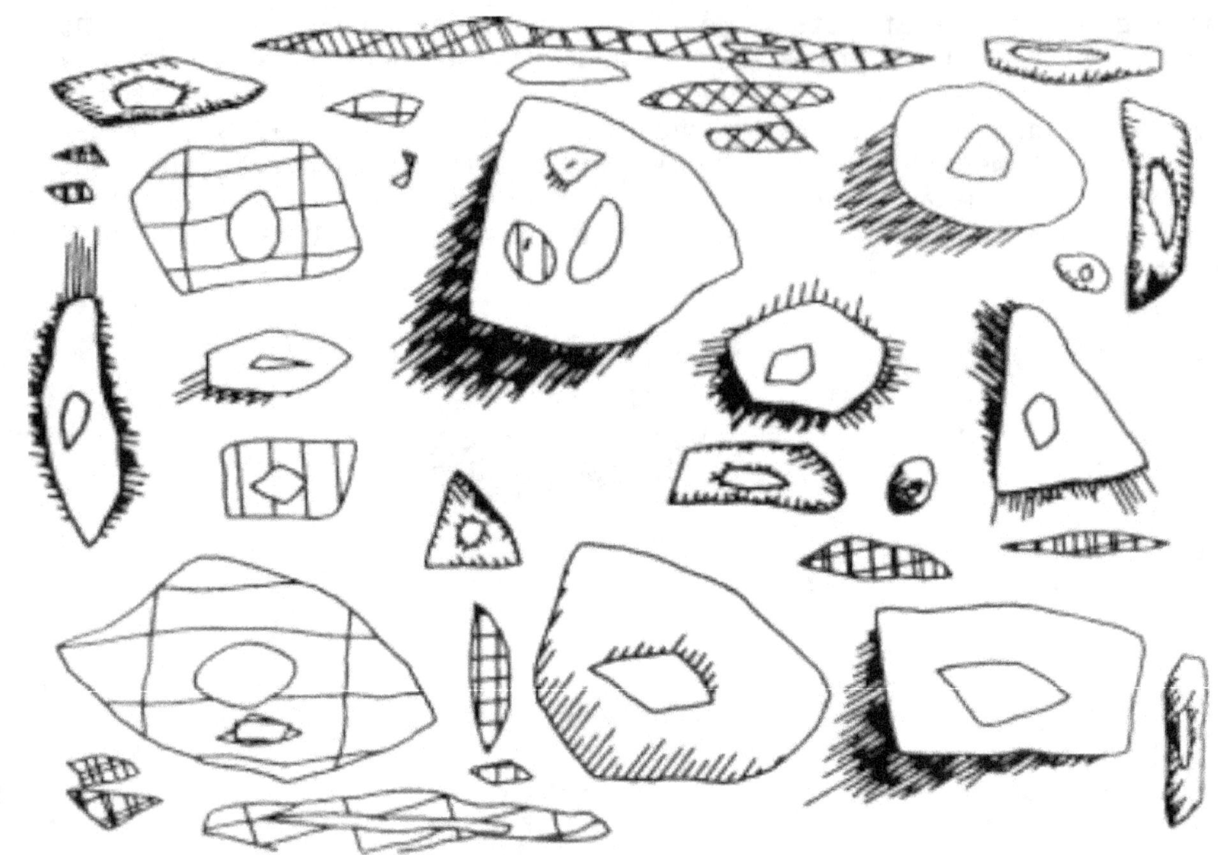

fig 12

But references to closure, to space-filling, and to repetition occur throughout
the production system in both the left and the right parts. They constitute,
not a set of rules so much as a set of protocols, the complex intertwin- ing
of which gives the entire program its particular identity. They are best con-
sidered as characterizing the program's world rather than as controlling how
the program is to behave within that world; as characterizing — if I risk
anthropomorphizing a little too far — what the program understands its world
to be like.

Space-filling and repetition are two of several protocols which have been add-
ed to the program since the outset, most of them simply extending upon the
initial ones. I mean that shading is a way of underlining the closedness of
a closed figure, and the program now knows a number of ways in which that can
be done (12). A recent extension to the figure-ground protocol requires the
program to respect the territorial integrity of previously drawn figures. This
one results in some of the more unpredictable and evocative configurations;
though it is never easy, even watching the drawings being done, to keep track
of what is causing what.

Adding a single new protocol to a program is more like adding a whole new con-
ceptual complex to a human's world model than it is like adding a new behav-
ioral rule, and it should not be surprising that the complexity of the draw-
ings increases rapidly for each added protocol. This seems to suggest that the
program structure is appropriate to the requirement of variety which I noted

earlier, since it seems unlikely that human output increases in variety only at the cost of extremely large rule-sets.

I have not yet had sufficient time working with a reasonably well-developed program to reach detailed conclusions on the nature of that variety, and on how the enmeshing of the different protocols produces it. But it does seem clear that it is the enmeshing, not the individual protocols, which is responsible. Note, for example, that although one drawing may exhibit more sophisticated space filling — shading — abilities than another, it will not have the same evocative force as a "simpler" drawing which exercises both open and closed protocols (cf 10,12). In fact, I think there is evidence to suggest that in the presence of closed forms, open forms take on a distinctly differentiat- ed function, providing a kind of semantic connective tissue for the semantical- ly dominant — more obviously object-like — closed forms. It is certainly the case that the spatial relatedness of the figures significantly affects their individual reading.

****

There is one further aspect to the program, having to do with task-oriented behavior rather than with perceptual behavior, which I should touch on briefly. It controls the way in which the program goes about the actual production, and the physical articulation, of the simulated freehand line from which the drawings are built.

I quickly came to the general conclusion, when I first became involved in com- puting, that human drawings are potentially interesting to human beings at least in large part because they have been made by other human beings; and that for a machine to inspire a similar kind of interest in its products it would have to make its drawings in the same sort of way that humans produce theirs. Of course, everything I have been talking about has been an effort to eluci- date what that "same sort of way" might be, but I am thinking now specifically about the lowest-level business of driving a pencil from one place to another.

What seemed certain to me, and still does, is that freehand drawing involves an elaborate feedback mechanism, a continuous matching of current state against desired end state and a continuous correction of deviation, essentially like the mechanisms we use to thread a needle, or drink a glass of water, or drive a car. Most of the time the feedback is required -- and the artist can claim no exemptions in this regard — by the unpredictability of the equipment we use, whether that unpredictability is caused by arthritis or worn bearings, lack of muscular coordination or sloppy steering. We do not optimize in freehand drawing, and it never seemed to me that the dynamic qualities of drawing would be captured by spline interpolations. Indeed, it never seemed to me that those qualities would be reproducible by trying to mimic appearance at all.

Imagine the problem of driving your car off a main road, where you are fac- ing in one direction, into a narrow drive- way at an arbitrary angle to it. Unless you would proceed by planning your whole course in advance and then closing your eyes and stepping on the gas, you will probably be doing very much what the program does. Given the task of getting from one place, facing in one direction, to another place and facing in another direction, it never knows how to accomplish the entire task, but "imagines" a series of temporary destinations, each of which will bring it a lit- tle closer to approaching its goal from the specified direction (13)' A degree of randomizing is provided as an analogue for arthritic joints, and as it never had any pre- cisely defined path to follow anyway it corrects for accu- mulating discrepancies only when they become big enough to jeopardize its chances of ever reaching its final destination.

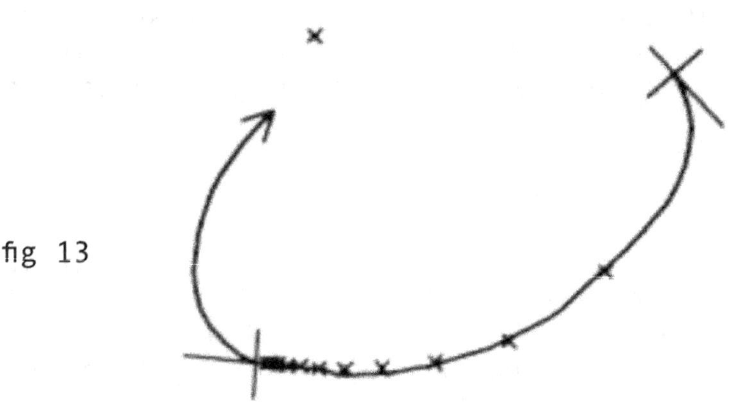

fig 13

It never knows in advance what will constitute a complete path, and it nev- er fails to complete its path. This part of the program is non-trivial, and certainly not optimal, involving as it does a complex series of decisions for every one of the small line segments which go into the building of a line. But I believe the simulation is a good one, and I have found it possible, moreover, to modify the character of the line — the artist's "handwriting" — by the ma- nipulation of such thoroughly practical factors as the rate at which sampling is done, the suddenness with which correction is applied, and the frequency with which the program sets up new "imagined" destinations along its path.

****

It seems to me that most of the things one might say about image-building might be said equally about image-reading. The reason for this, I think, is that the element common to both — the propensity for attaching significance to events, for endowing entities with identities — is also an overwhelmingly important one. It is not the unique property of artists, obviously.

This is not to say that the identity which the viewer at- taches to a complex of marks is exclusively a function of the viewer's propensity, or even that any complex of marks would serve equally well to trigger that propensity. The natural world is full of complex forms, and if we sometimes play with them -- clouds, for example — we are well aware that their "meanings" are our own invention. Marks which we recognize as being man-made, on the other hand, -- and in particular those man-made marks which we see as arising from an intent on the part of the maker to communicate -- these we treat in a special way, not merely assigning significance to them but insisting that that significance has been carried by the marks themselves.

I believe that in searching images for evidence of their origins the mind is surprisingly literalistic. If a machine program is able to produce image-rich material, it does so by virtue of persuading the viewer that the maker was a human being living in a human world, and that his intent was to communicate something about that world. The assumption of intentionality precedes the "re-construction" of intent.

In this case the simulated perceptual mechanisms give evidence of the under-lying humanness of the drawing's manufacture and the drawer's world — though perhaps any other set of reasonably low-level mechanisms would have served equally well — and the constant complex decision-making which actually takes place, and which is clearly evident in the articulation of the line, confirms the viewer's belief in the artist's intentionality.

This conclusion is not adequate to account for the more highly particularized readings which seem to attach to the drawings — notably the humor and the sense of narrative — and I do not know at this stage how they are to be accounted for.

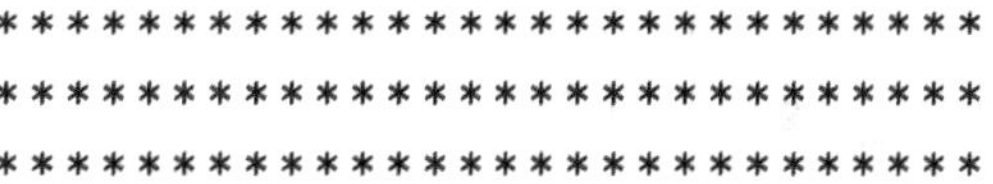

It became evident from the questions and the private discussions which fol-lowed this paper that my use of the label "protocol" had done more to confuse than to elucidate the conceptual unit to which I had applied it. Reviewing that usage, it becomes apparent that my understanding of what the program is doing — what roles the different elements in its structure play — has shifted with time, and I have been careless enough to carry over to a slowly emerging construct a term inappropriate to it, but unfortunately still more or less appropriate to something else. The underlying confusion has been my own, of course, and I am glad to have been presented with this opportunity to try to resolve it.

Given the choice between rewriting the paper and extending it with a post-script-ed commentary, I have chosen the lat- ter course. This gives me the chance also to deal in a more measured fashion with one particular question which is evidently quite troubling to a good many people.

* *

I suggest above that what I call a protocol is best regarded as characteriz-ing what the program understands its world to be like, not as a rule which controls how it is to behave in that world. A rule is expressed within the program by a production. A protocol is not fully expressed by a production. I would not want to change any of this — except the use of the word "protocol" itself — but the problem is that nothing has been said about the structure, or what we might call the dynamics, of the characterization. In the absence of any overview clearly differentiated from the rule-oriented schema to which the characterization must obviously relate, the mere assertion that a protocol is not simply a rule is hardly sufficient to expunge the sense that it is. So be it: let me return "protocol" to the rule-oriented domain whence it came. In its place, and hopefully more fully expressive of the conceptual complex it is meant to carry, I will use the term "epimorph".

An epimorph characterizes what the program understands its world to be like, and the machine draws in a human, or quasi-human, fashion because its set of epimorphs are closely modeled on human epimorphs. We might go as far as to say that it exercises a subset of human epimorphs. In dealing with the dynamics of the characterization process, then — and thus in attempting to elucidate what an epi- morph is — it may prove more revealing to consider an example of human, rather than machine, performance. Here is one taken from the drawing class mentioned earlier.

A brief background account is in order.

Two weeks into a deliberately dislocative class — people bring such rigidly formulated notions about drawing to a beginning class! — one struggling student volunteered the view that drawing was, as far as he could tell, "just a question of getting from one point to another". Always happy to take what is offered, I proposed that in that case they might get into the business of drawing more freely if they didn't have to worry about the points. Each of them could provide an array of dots for someone else, who would then only have to figure out how to get from one to another.

In practice, it required fairly rigorous measures to ensure that these dot arrays did not carry any representational weight of their own to constrain subsequent performance. Eventually we had two sets of drawings, thirty-four in all, pinned up for examination, and before any discussion began I asked the students whether they could write down the rules which they had followed in joining up the dots. They all wrote down the same three rules! — 1. see if you can see an image in the dots, and if so draw a line around it: 2. if you can't see an image, draw closed figures anyway: and, 3. if you can't do 1 or 2, fake it. "Faking it", on questioning, turned out to mean using open structures like short straight lines, zigzags, and so on, as space filling.

Examination of the drawings themselves showed that there were several other rules of a more surprising kind operating. Consider that any dot in an array might potentially become the junction of an indeterminate number of lines joining it to any number of other dots. Of the simpler cases, the order-two case denotes a dot on a continuous line, the order-one case marks the end of a line, and the null case is a dot which has not been joined up to anything.

Karin's "eyes" would be an example of the null case.

Since the drawings all contained between a hundred and two hundred dots, we might guess that there would be considerable variety in the numbers of lines joining at these junc- tions: in fact, we found only three cases of order-four, and only two cases of order-more-than-four, junctions, in the entire set of thirty-four drawings. Over 99.5 t> of the dots had three lines or less attached to them! (A similar situation will be observed in the drawings of both Karin and Sherry, figures 3 and 4.)

The students were certainly unaware, until it was pointed out to them, that their behavior had been constrained in this way, and were even a little resentful of the suggestion that they had done anything according to rules of any sort. Yet, curiously enough, there were a few cases where "extra" dots had occurred when two lines had been allowed to cross, and in all these cases the students concerned reported a strong sense of having done something wrong, broken some powerful though unstated rule. The class as a whole evidently recognized an unstated interdiction against crossing lines also, and unanimously agreed that these "extra" dots should not be counted as order-four junctions.

Consistent though this behavioral pattern was, it only required attention to be focused upon it for It to change. The discussion which followed the making of these drawings evidently identified "junctionality" as an issue, and although nothing was said about what might constitute acceptable behavior in relation to this issue, the drawings which followed in subsequent weeks all contained a much richer distribution of order-more-than-four junctions; we discovered also that their use involved increasingly com- plex, but hardly less consistent, rule-sets than we had found at the beginning.

We need not go into detail here on the precise nature of these new rules. The point is that they could all be described by a production-like paradigm involving as- sessment of the current state of the drawing — in relation to junctionality among other things ~ on the left side, and some action resulting in a change of state — through the manipulation of junctionality among other things — on the right side. The notion of junctionality itself would not be adequately expressed by any one of these productions, however, and it clearly exists on a "higher" heirar- chical level than that of the individual productions. It has become one of the issues which the student believes to be significant in relation to the domain of drawing, and thus characterizes what he believes that domain to be like. It is in this sense isomorphic with those other issues of territoriality, openness/closedness, containment and re- petition, which I said characterized what the program understood its world to be like. It will be clear from this account that of these, at least openness/ closedness is also an active epimorph for the human: but I am sure that more extensive evidence will be found in a wide variety of material, and in domains not limited to drawing activity.

****

One of the questions I was asked — not for the first time, by any means — was: am I proposing that the machine pro- gram constitutes a model of human creative behavior? Is it a sort of automated surrogate Harold Cohen?

A full answer would go far beyond my present scope — and, indeed, my present abilities -- and would involve all those other troubling philosophical questions which the existence of the computer inevitably raises. A short answer would be that human beings live in a real world, and their internal representations of that world include reference to its objects: the current state of the program knows nothing of the real world or of its objects. Human beings learn from experience: the program begins each new drawing without any memory of previous drawings, and with its production system unmodified by having made them. In these and in other respects the machine's performance is not merely less than, but is unlike, human performance. It should be stressed, however, that these are limitations in the current state of this program, and are not to be regarded as intrinsic to programs in general.

Most searching questions about the nature of the machine turn out to be questions about the nature of people, and this one is no exception. Before we could venture a more complete answer we would need to consider what we really mean by creative behavior, for if that is to be judged exclusively in terms of the manifest results of its exercise — we know so-and-so is creative because he makes a great many original images — then clearly the machine is extremely creative. It's drawings are probably as good, as original, as any I ever made myself, and I am hopelessly outclassed by it in terms of productivity.

But once we have stripped off these layers of the artist's activity which have to do with marketable objects, with the desire for approval, for fame or for notoriety, with propa- ganda for this religious belief or that economic system: once, in short, we have stripped off the artist's public and cultural functions, how will we characterize the remaining private, essentially self-serving, functions? What does the artist make images for?

My own view can be stated briefly and without oversim- plifying too far. I believe that the artist is engaged, as everybody else is, in building internal representations of his world, and that his behavior is remarkable in only two major respects. The first — and this seems to me to be a feature common to art-making, science-doing, philosophy, mathematics, and most other higher intellectual pursuits — is that the formulating and continuous reformulating of mental models is carried on as a foreground, and as a highly structured, activity: not as a background activity. The second is that he exhibits a high level of preoccupa- tion with the structure of representation as such.

In neither of these respects does he require special mental equipment, and indeed I would assume that the cultural value of his activity, the extraordinary regard in which images are held, rests upon the fundamental normality of the mental functions exercised. I mean that the basic structure of all internal model building is the assignment of associative reference: what we might call the "standing-for-ness" principle. We would not be going too far to regard art as an endless explorative game built around the presumably universally human fact that things can stand for other things.

The playing out of this game produces images, normally embodied in objects, which may be valued by the culture for any of a number of reasons. For the artist, it is the play- ing out of the game, and thus the making of the ob- ject — rather than the object itself — which is important. If object-making is the means to an end, the end is not the object — art objects are interesting to the degree that they stand for something outside themselves — but the continuous development of new moves in the game. Externaliza- tion is a part of the artist's methodology in the building of internal representations of his world: a world which includes representations as a central feature.

We are now in a position to generate a slightly more com- plete answer to the original question, and I think we will find that the view which the question proposed — that the program is an artificial artist capable of creative behav- ior — is both more than and less than adequate. The program does not develop new game-states: it plays the legal moves in the current game. It says "Let me tell you about my world", but rich though that world may be, the telling does not result in any further enrichment. We thus have no reason to say that the machine has any interest in the one feature I have chosen to regard as fundamental to human art-making — the continuous development of the in- ternal representation of the world.

To this degree, it is clearly an inadequate model of human performance: which is not to say that no program could ever provide an adequate one. On the other hand, it does not merely model the playing of legal moves in the game, it actu- ally plays them. To this degree the program is not a model of human performance at all. It carries out a real, and rather extensive, part of the art-making procedure, and its output is in every important respect interchangeable — both culturally and privately — with output which might result from more orthodox art-making procedures. MY world changes as a result of the program telling about it, and in the long term the program changes also. I assume from this that I will go on working on the one program indefinitely, without ever feeling the need to abandon it and start on a completely new one.

Some caution is in order. I have reached this point in many conversations to be told "Oh, you mean that the computer is just a tool." The answer to this is that the advent of the electronic computer requires a total rethinking of what tools might be, for if the thermostat and the speed governor are exactly equivalent to biological feedback systems, com- puter programs are potentially exactly equivalent to intellectual feedback systems. We have a long way to go before we fully comprehend the shift in significance of "tools" capable of the independent exercise of reason.

I have said several times that the limitations attaching to this program should not be regarded as fundamental limitations in programs. I do not know what will change, for example, or how they will change, when this program does have some knowledge of the world, and can make decisions about the drawing in terms of that knowledge: or when it can use its memory of past drawings as a determinant in building new ones.

Prediction is a hazardous game, and I will limit myself here to only one. I do not believe that any program will ever produce art unless it was written by an artist — as the words have been defined by this discussion — and its running serves a vital role for that individual in the changing patterns of his internal model building. The Sci-Fi fantasy of putting an artist's "genius" on tape and flooding the world with his work after his death, or of becoming a great composer in the twentieth century by wri- ting a program to generate Bach: these merely reflect the confusion of art with its objects.

****

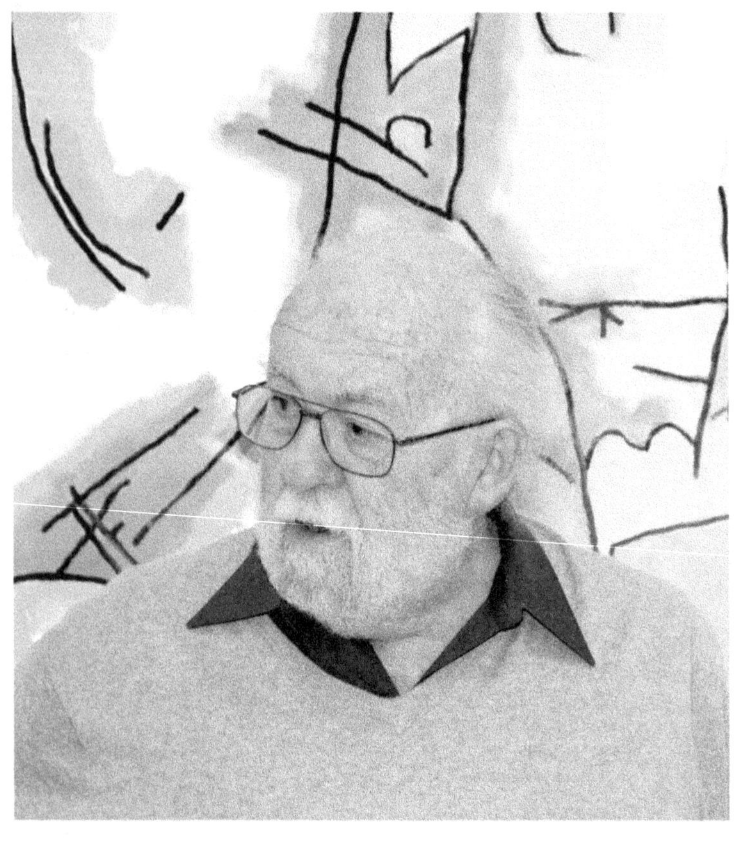

HAROLD COHEN (1928-2016) won a major reputation as a painter in London in the 1960s, representing the UK in the Venice Biennale, documenta 4 and many other international art venues. In 1968 he left London for the University of California, San Diego and there met his first computer. By 1972, as a guest scholar at Stanford University's AI Lab, he had embarked upon the project that would occupy him for the next forty-plus years, his now-celebrated AARON program. Since then, and working to bring computing into the mainstream of art, he has exhibited widely with AARON: the Tate Gallery, the LA County Museum, the Stedelijk in Amsterdam, the San Francisco Museum, documenta 6 and many other major public spaces, using his own purpose-built drawing and painting machines as well as his Fingerpainting System for the 21st Century. He has also shown in Science Museums across the US, most notably the Museum of Computing History, which now has a permanent exhibit devoted to his work.

Cohen has contributed more than thirty theoretical essays, invited conference papers and public lectures, to the field, most of them freely available through his website, haroldcohen.com. In 2014 he was honored with a Distinguished Artist Award for Lifetime Achievement in Digital Arts. He retired from UCSD in 1994 but continued his collaborative efforts with Aaron in Encinitas California until his passing in April 2016.

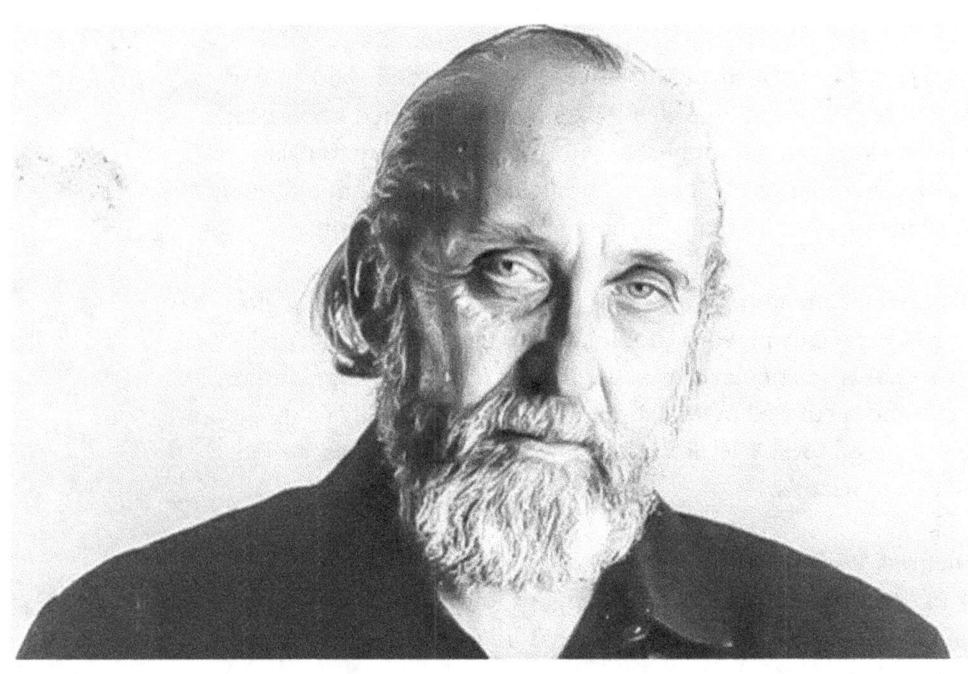

is an internationally celebrated poet, translator, anthologist, and performer with over ninety books of poetry and twelve assemblages of traditional and avant-garde poetry such as *Technicians of the Sacred, Shaking the Pumpkin* (traditional American Indian poetry), *Exiled in the Word* (a.k.a. A Big Jewish Book), and, with Pierre Joris and Jeffrey Robinson, *Poems for the Millennium*, volumes 1-3. He was a founding figure of ethnopoetics as a combination of poetic practice and theory, and he has been a longtime practitioner and theorist of poetry performance. His most recent big books are *Eye of Witness: A Jerome Rothenberg Reader* (2013) and *Barbaric Vast & Wild: Outside & Subterranean Poetry from Origins to Preset* (volume 5 of *Poems for the Millennium*, 2015). A new book of poems, *A Field on Mars: Poems 2000-2015*, has recently appeared in separate English and French editions.

The Operating System's *Glossarium: Unsilenced Texts* series was established in early 2016 in an effort to amplify and recover silenced voices outside and buried underneath the familiar poetic canon, seeking out and publishing both contemporary translations and little known (and unknown) out of print texts, in particular those under siege by restrictive regimes and silencing practices in their home (or adoptive) countries.

The term "Glossarium" derives from latin/greek and is defined as "a collection of glosses or explanations of words, especially of words not in general use, as those of a dialect, locality or an art or science, or of particular words used by an old or a foreign author." The series was initiated by and is curated by Managing Editor Lynne DeSilva-Johnson, with the help of contributing editors Ariel Resnikoff and Stephen Ross, as well as a wide range of global allies and friends.

Ashraf Fayadh's "Instructions Within," in a full Arabic-English dual-language translation, was the first book in this new series, preceding Gregory Randall's award winning memoir of life in Cuba, *"To Have Been There Then (Estar Allí Entonces).*

Three additional parallel Spanish-English translations by Margaret Randall follow in 2017-18—Chely Lima's *"Lo Que Les Dijo El Licántropo / What the Werewolf Told Them,"* a special edition of Rita Valdivia's poetry, *"La Comandante Maya,"* (published in commemoration of the 50th anniversary of the death of Che Guevara in Bolivia) and *"Viaje de Regreso / Return Trip,"* Cuban poet Israel Dominguez's striking poetry, with a beautiful cover featuring Havana street art by Jose Parla and JR.

2018 will also see a dual language Farsi-English edition of *The Book of Sounds* by Mehdi Navid, translated by Tina Rahimi, with original cover art by Iman Raad.

The fall of 2017 also saw the publication of the book in your hands: the expanded edition of the out of print 1984 collaborative text, (15) *Flower World Variations,* by poet Jerome Rothenberg and groundbreaking digital artist Harold Cohen, originally produced as a limited edition from Membrane Press. Breathing new life into highly innovative projects like this one is central to the mission of The OS as well as to the *Glossarium* series—in particular when we have the opportunity to add archival material to the content (and the record). We hope you enjoy this wonderful edition and encourage you to be in touch about potential projects for this series to amplify!

*The Operating System uses the language "print document" to differentiate from the book-object as part of our mission to distinguish the act of documentation-in-book-FORM from the act of publishing as a backwards facing replication of the book's agentive *role* as it may have appeared the last several centuries of its history. Ultimately, I approach the book as TECHNOLOGY: one of a variety of printed documents (in this case bound) that humans have invented and in turn used to archive and disseminate ideas, beliefs, stories, and other evidence of production.*

Ownership and use of printing presses and access to (or restriction of printed materials) has long been a site of struggle, related in many ways to revolutionary activity and the fight for civil rights and free speech all over the world. While (in many countries) the contemporary quotidian landscape has indeed drastically shifted in its access to platforms for sharing information and in the widespread ability to "publish" digitally, even with extremely limited resources, the importance of publication on physical media has not diminished. In fact, this may be the most critical time in recent history for activist groups, artists, and others to insist upon learning, establishing, and encouraging personal and community documentation practices.

With The OS's print endeavors I wanted to open up a conversation about this: the ultimately radical, transgressive act of creating PRINT /DOCUMENTATION in the digital age. It's a question of the archive, and of history: who gets to tell the story, and what evidence of our life, our behaviors, our experiences are we leaving behind? We can know little to nothing about the future into which we're leaving an unprecedentedly digital document trail—but we can be assured that publications, government agencies, museums, schools, and other institutional powers that be will continue to leave BOTH a digital and print version of their production for the official record. Will we?

As a (rogue) anthropologist and long time academic, I can easily pull up many accounts about how lives, behaviors, experiences—how THE STORY of a time or place—was pieced together using the deep study of correspondence, notebooks, and other physical documents which are no longer the norm in many lives and practices. As we move our creative behaviors towards digital note taking, and even audio and video, what can we predict about future technology that is in any way assuring that our stories will be accurately told—or told at all? How will we leave these things for the record?

In these documents we say:
WE WERE HERE, WE EXISTED, WE HAVE A DIFFERENT STORY

— Lynne DeSilva-Johnson, Founder/Managing Editor,
THE OPERATING SYSTEM, Brooklyn NY 2016

An Absence So Great and Spontaneous It Is Evidence of Light - Anne Gorrick [2018]
Chlorosis   - Michael Flatt and Derrick Mund [2018]
Sussuros a Mi Padre - Erick Sáenz [2018]
Sharing Plastic - Blake Nemec [2018]
The Book of Sounds - Mehdi Navid (Farsi dual language, trans. Tina Rahimi) [2018]
In Corpore Sano : Creative Practice and the Challenged Body
[Anthology, 2018] Lynne DeSilva-Johnson and Jay Besemer, co-editors
Abandoners - Lesley Ann Wheeler [2018]
Jazzercise is a Language - Gabriel Ojeda-Sague [2018]
Death is a Festival - Anis Shivani [2018]
Return Trip / Viaje Al Regreso; Dual Language Edition -
Israel Dominguez,(trans. Margaret Randall) [2018]
Born Again - Ivy Johnson [2018]
Singing for Nothing - Wally Swist [2018]

One More Revolution - Andrea Mazzariello [2017]
Fugue State Beach - Filip Marinovich [2017]
Lost City Hydrothermal Field - Peter Milne Greiner [2017]
The Book of Everyday Instruction - Chloe Bass [2017]
An Exercise in Necromancy - Patrick Roche [Bowery Poetry Imprint, 2017]
Love, Robot - Margaret Rhee[2017]
La Comandante Maya - Rita Valdivia (dual language, trans. Margaret Randall) [2017]
The Furies - William Considine [2017]
Nothing Is Wasted - Shabnam Piryaei [2017]
Mary of the Seas - Joanna C. Valente [2017]
Secret-Telling Bones - Jessica Tyner Mehta [2017]
CHAPBOOK SERIES 2017 : INCANTATIONS
featuring original cover art by Barbara Byers
sp. - Susan Charkes; Radio Poems - Jeffrey Cyphers Wright; Fixing a Witch/Hexing the Stitch
- Jacklyn Janeksela; cosmos a personal voyage by carl sagan ann druyan steven sotor and me -
Connie Mae Oliver
Flower World Variations, Expanded Edition/Reissue - Jerome
Rothenberg and Harold Cohen [2017]
What the Werewolf Told Them / Lo Que Les Dijo El Licantropo -
Chely Lima (trans. Margaret Randall) [2017]
The Color She Gave Gravity - Stephanie Heit [2017]
The Science of Things Familiar - Johnny Damm [Graphic Hybrid, 2017]
agon - Judith Goldman [2017]
To Have Been There Then / Estar Alli Entonces - Gregory Randall
(trans. Margaret Randall) [2017]

Instructions Within - Ashraf Fayadh [2016]
Arabic-English dual language edition; Mona Kareem, translator
Let it Die Hungry - Caits Meissner [2016]
A GUN SHOW - Adam Sliwinski and Lynne DeSilva-Johnson;
So Percussion in Performance with Ain Gordon and Emily Johnson [2016]
Everybody's Automat [2016] - Mark Gurarie
How to Survive the Coming Collapse of Civilization [2016] - Sparrow
CHAPBOOK SERIES 2016: OF SOUND MIND
*featuring the quilt drawings of Daphne Taylor
Improper Maps - Alex Crowley; While Listening - Alaina Ferris;
Chords - Peter Longofono; Any Seam or Needlework - Stanford Cheung

TEN FOUR - Poems, Translations, Variations [2015]- Jerome Rothenberg, Ariel
Resnikoff, Mikhl Likht
MARILYN [2015] - Amanda Ngoho Reavey
CHAPBOOK SERIES 2015: OF SYSTEMS OF
*featuring original cover art by Emma Steinkraus
Cyclorama - Davy Knittle; The Sensitive Boy Slumber Party Manifesto
- Joseph Cuillier; Neptune Court - Anton Yakovlev; Schema - Anurak Saelow
SAY/MIRROR [2015; 2nd edition 2016] - JP HOWARD
Moons Of Jupiter/Tales From The Schminke Tub [plays, 2014] - Steve Danziger

CHAPBOOK SERIES 2014: BY HAND
Pull, A Ballad - Maryam Parhizkar; Can You See that Sound - Jeff Musillo
Executive Producer Chris Carter - Peter Milne Grenier;
Spooky Action at a Distance - Gregory Crosby;

CHAPBOOK SERIES 2013: WOODBLOCK
*featuring original prints from Kevin William Reed
Strange Coherence - Bill Considine; The Sword of Things - Tony Hoffman;
Talk About Man Proof - Lancelot Runge / John Kropa; An Admission as a Warning
Against the Value of Our Conclusions -Alexis Quinlan

DOC U MENT
/däkyəmənt/

First meant "instruction" or "evidence," whether written or not.

noun - a piece of written, printed, or electronic matter that provides information or evidence or that serves as an official record
verb - record (something) in written, photographic, or other form
synonyms - paper - deed - record - writing - act - instrument

[*Middle English, precept, from Old French, from Latin documentum, example, proof, from docre, to teach; see dek- in Indo-European roots.*]

Who is responsible for the manufacture of value?

Based on what supercilious ontology have we landed in a space
where we vie against other creative people
in vain pursuit of the fleeting credibilities of the scarcity economy,
rather than freely collaborating and sharing openly with each other
in ecstatic celebration of MAKING?

While we understand and acknowledge the economic pressures and fear-mongering
that threatens to dominate and crush the creative impulse,
we also believe that ***now more than ever
we have the tools to relinquish agency via cooperative means,***
fueled by the fires of the Open Source Movement.

**Looking out across the invisible vistas of that rhizomatic parallel country
we can begin to see our community beyond constraints,
in the place where intention meets
resilient, proactive, collaborative organization.**

Here is a document born of that belief, sown purely of imagination and will.
When we document we assert.
We print to make real, to reify our being there.
When we do so with mindful intention to address our process,
to open our work to others, to create beauty in words in space,
to respect and acknowledge the strength of the page we now hold physical,
a thing in our hand… we remind ourselves that, like Dorothy:
we had the power all along, my dears.

THE PRINT! DOCUMENT SERIES
is a project of
the trouble with bartleby
in collaboration with
the operating system